Prophets, Prophecy, & Prophetic Gifting

Rev. Michael Fram

Prophets, Prophecy, & Prophetic Gifting

Prophets, Prophecy, & Prophetic Gifting.

Copyright © 2024 by Rev. Michael Fram.

First Edition.

Print ISBN: 978-0-9843003-6-5

eBook ISBN: 978-0-9843003-7-2

Cover Design: David Munoz Prophetic Art.

www.DavidMunozArts.com

Published by Prophetic Destiny Ministries.

Copyediting and formatting, L3 Editorial Services

All rights reserved. No part of this book may be reproduced or transmitted in any form or by any means without written permission of the author, except in brief quotes or reviews.

Unless otherwise noted, all scriptures are from the NEW KING JAMES VERSION® (NKJV).. Copyright© 1982 by Thomas Nelson, Inc. Used by permission. All rights reserved.

Scripture quotations marked (KJV) are taken from the KING JAMES VERSION, public domain.

Scriptures marked AMPC are taken from the Amplified® Bible Classic, Copyright © 1954, 1958, 1962, 1964, 1965, 1987 by The Lockman Foundation. Used by permission. www.Lockman.org

Scripture quotations marked MSG are taken from THE MESSAGE, copyright © 1993, 2002, 2018 by Eugene H. Peterson. Used by permission of NavPress. All rights reserved. Represented by Tyndale House Publishers, a Division of Tyndale House Ministries.

Scripture quotations noted as NASB are taken from the NEW AMERICAN STANDARD BIBLE®, Copyright ©1960, 1962, 1963, 1968, 1971, 1972, 1973, 1975, 1977, 1995 by The Lockman Foundation. Used by permission.

Scripture quotations marked (NLT) are taken from the Holy Bible, New Living Translation, copyright ©1996, 2004, 2015 by Tyndale House

Foundation. Used by permission of Tyndale House Publishers, Carol Stream, Illinois 60188. All rights reserved.

All dictionary word definitions contained within this work are sourced from Webster's Online Dictionary.. Merriam-Webster.com

Contents

Endorsements ix
Foreword xvii
Preface xix
Introduction xxiii

1. From The Beginning: Prophecy vs. Prophets 1
2. The Gift Of Prophecy 6
3. Beginning To Flow In Prophecy 37
4. Following Protocol 47
5. Flowing In And Receiving From The Prophetic 59
6. Levels Of Prophetic Gifting 78
7. The Office Of The Prophet 83
8. Special Areas Of The Prophetic 98
9. Unrealistic Expectations Of The Prophetic 109
10. Sonship: A Missing Element In The Prophetic 115
11. The Synergistic Working Of Apostles & Prophets 128

Final Thoughts 137
About the Author 139
Also by Rev. Michael Fram 141

Endorsements

In *Prophets, Prophecy, & Prophetic Gifting,* Apostle Michael Fram dives deep into the intricate world of prophecy, providing a clear roadmap for those wishing to understand or develop their prophetic gift. The book thoughtfully distinguishes between the roles of prophets and the act of prophecy, before offering guidance on how one can begin to navigate the prophetic realm.

Through chapters such as "Following Protocol" and "Flowing In And Receiving From The Prophetic," readers are equipped with practical tools to ensure they are both giving and receiving prophetic messages in alignment with divine principles.

Fram's discussion on the symbiotic relationship between apostles and prophets in the final chapter solidifies the book's comprehensive approach to the subject. A standout is Chapter 10, which sheds light on the vital element of 'sonship' often overlooked in prophetic circles.

This book is not just for the spiritually inclined, but for anyone seeking to understand the prophetic dimension of their faith more deeply. The richness of its insights is why everyone needs to have a copy on their bookshelf.

> Apostle Barry Cook, Houston TX USA
> Leaders Edge Training Inc.
> *Establishing Your Course Through The Prophetic Anointing.*
> *Mission Minded Leaders*
> Amazon.com

Apostle Michael Fram is a seasoned man of the word of God and a friend of mine since 2013. Our relationship began as an acquaintance on Facebook, then it moved into phone calls with each other, to ultimately doing video teachings together over the last several years on several important subjects much needed in the body of Christ.

Now we minister together across the nation, and are both Senior Council members with a rapidly growing movement in the US, Canada, the Philippines and abroad.

Michael Fram is a seasoned instructor when it comes to the Word of God. He wields the scalpel (the two-edged sword) as good as anybody I know. His line upon line teaching and instruction is par excellent.

His years of study and research on this manuscript's topic qualify him to pen what Holy Spirit has downloaded to him over the last few decades.

There has been tremendous misunderstanding, wrong concepts, and mindsets about Prophets, Prophecy, and Prophetic Gifts.

Michael's book will pull back the veil on the false, the misunderstood, and the error to bring tremendous balance back to this much needed subject, especially in the day and hour that we are living in. Read it the first time, then get your Bible and notebook out and study it the second time. Your life will be forever changed.

I am honored to call him my friend and Kingdom brother, I affectionately call him "Bubba."

Dr. Don Hughes
Founder of RHSOM
(Rev House School of Ministry)
Apostolic Leader of
Rev House Fellowship
Senior Council Member of Love & Unity

Apostle Michael Fram is my brother in Christ. He is affectionately known as 'Apostle Mike' and we call each other 'lighter twin and darker twin' respectively.

I met Mike in 1994 in our twin island republic of Trinidad and Tobago. He first came to our country as an Evangelist. He came to visit his parents, Papa Leo and

Mama Edith Fram, who were interim presidents of Caribbean Mission Bible School – my alma mater.

Mike and I shared over the years on the prophetic and apostolic ministry. His new book, *Prophets, Prophecy, & Prophetic Gifting* delivers spiritual edification and empowerment to the body of Christ. An endorsement of this text dispels the darkness of ignorance endeavoring to shroud the truth of the five-fold ministry at this time. It's not 'hearsay,' because Michael Fram serves in an Apostolic Prophetic capacity. He is the Nabi Prophetic stream while I am the Seer stream of the prophetic mantle.

Apostle Mike wisely included, "Sonship – A Missing Element in the Prophetic." I quote, *"We really do need more mature prophetic mothers and fathers to arise and pour into up-and-coming prophetic voices, and those with blossoming prophetic gifts."* This should be shouted from the rooftops of our churches. I thank God for my brother Mike and endorse this rich resource as an encouragement to any young as well as senior prophet to procure and meditate on Prophets, Prophecy, & Prophetic Gifting.

Prophets, Prophecy, & Prophetic Gifting is an excellent training manual for the School of the Prophets. Well written, Apostle Mike!

Apostle, Dr. Christopher Douglas
Liberty Apostolic Ministries Network
Trinidad, WI

It is my honor and privilege to write this endorsement for Apostle Michael Fram's newest book: *Prophets, Prophecy, & Prophetic Gifting*. Michael presents clear and precise principles drawn from over four decades of experience as both a Prophet and a Teacher. These Biblical principles, together with Michael's personal anecdotes, join precept with illustration in a way that will drive the Truth home to every hungry heart that reads this book.

One specific principle that must be kept in mind is that prophetic utterances are conditional (*Jeremiah 18:7-10*). The preface sets forth specific goals that this book should accomplish. It is with the greatest joy and appreciation that it can be declared to Apostle Michael, "Mission Accomplished!"

Love and Blessings to you, my Brother!

Dr. Jefferson K. Thompson
Fresh Water Ministries, International
Pineville, LA USA

As fellow Rhema graduates and ministry colleagues over the course of several decades, I can attest to the great passion Micheal has for Jesus, His Word, and His people. In *Prophets, Prophecy, & Prophetic Gifting*, he bestows on us a treasure trove of knowledge and personal experience to better our understanding of one of the most controversial subjects in the Church today. It is foundational in its approach, jam-packed with scripture and practical wisdom for how prophets and prophecy can optimally function as the priceless blessing they were designed to be. I especially applaud his use of storytelling to bolster the content, making this an easy and enjoyable read.

A beautiful characteristic of Michael's ministry is the way in which he honors and advocates for every member of Christ's body to flourish in their gifts, ensuring no one is overlooked or left behind. Reflected in this book is the heart of that mission, making certain everyone is equipped to release prophecy properly and powerfully, the voice of Jesus Christ in the earth.

Apostle Kathy Bichsel
Kathy Bichsel Ministries
kathybichsel.com
Author of *The Radical Rising Remnant*
Liberty Corner, New Jersey USA

Thank you Reverend Michael for this clear and concise teaching on *Prophets, Prophecy, & Prophetic Gifting,*. This book is a valuable tool for those seasoned in the faith and those who are curious and want to learn more about the prophetic realm. Superbly written, wonderfully researched, and a must-read to help the reader understand this precious gift the Lord desires us to pursue.

Margie Fleurant
President of Margie Fleurant Ministries.
Martinsville, New Jersey USA

Dedication

This book is dedicated to some Generals of the Faith and Authors that really spoke into my life through their ministries and books, particularly in the areas of the Gifts of The Spirit, and the Five-Fold Ministry early on in my ministry and training from the 80s through the 90s: Rev. Kenneth E. "Dad" Hagin and Dr. Lester Sumrall.

Prophetic Pioneers like Dr. Bill Hamon and Prophet Graham Cooke, whose books also made a great impact on my life and ministry starting around the year 2000 for the next several years. Without any of these men of God I would not be who I am, nor would I have the understanding of Prophets, Prophecy, or Prophetic Gifting.

Foreword

It is my honor to write this foreword and endorse this new manuscript for my oldest natural born son. This is a very unique book in that the author has combined personal illustrations and examples with sound Biblical teaching. By carefully blending these two styles together he has produced a very readable document that is easy to follow while remaining very interesting.

He begins with his very first encounter with the Holy Ghost when he was a teenager in high school. From that beginning he shares some of the experiences and people that have helped him to grow and develop into a mature servant of God. The scripture says iron sharpens iron, and Michael was blessed to have men like Dr. Kenneth E "Dad" Hagin and Pastor Billy Joe Daugherty speak into his life and help to sharpen him.

Michael takes on several of the topics that have been debated for many years. in Christian circles. He takes the time to present the issue, then gives some Biblical texts that deal with that subject. After presenting sound Exegesis of the scriptures he presents his conclusion. Anyone reading this book will have no doubt about where Michael stands on these controversial issues. He plainly lays out his ideas in everyday simple language. I for one am very pleased that he did not straddle the fence on any issue.

The section on levels of prophetic gifting is necessary teaching in the modern-day church. Many saints are gifted to release prophecies in our churches, but not all at the same level. Some are just beginning to flow in this gift, others have developed to a higher level, and still others have been called to stand in the Ministry Office of the Prophet. There is a huge difference between the 'word' of a novice and the word of a mature, seasoned minister. It is important to remember that all Prophets prophesy, but not all who prophesy are Prophets. It is required that every person learns the level of their personal prophetic gifting and is content to flow at that level, while seeking mentors who will help them develop into a higher level.

Dr. Leo Fram
President
Living Faith Ministries Int'l.
Living Faith Ministries Apostolic Network.
Brick, New Jersey USA

Preface

Do we really need another book on the Prophetic? I know…right?! I can hear many ask this question. Sadly, yes we do. For all the advances we have made in the last 35 – 40 years that the church at large has been evolving in this Prophetic Restoration that we have, it seems we still have miles to go.

I heard a statement recently by a dear brother and friend, Apostle Calvin Cook, he exclaimed: "It was not Prophecy on Demand in the Scripture, it was Prophecy on Command!" Let that sink in!

So why me? Why am I writing this book? Why now? These are all valid questions. To be honest, I have been working on this book on and off for over 10 years. I have started and stopped this book many times. I have added to it along the way. I have edited it and corrected it many times through the years.

I have been operating in the Manifestation Gift of Prophecy since I was 15 years old, and I am now 62 years old at the time of the publishing of this manuscript. If my Math is right that is 48 years that I have been prophesying. Out of the 4+ decades that I have been operating in ministry, (45 years) as of the publishing of this book, I functioned as an Ascension Gift Prophet for 16 of them.

When I first had this book drop in my spirit some 10+ years ago, many of the things that needed to be corrected then, still need to be corrected now!

As I look at where we are I realize:

- We need to learn the difference between the Manifestation Gift of Prophecy and the Ministry Gift of Prophet.
- We need to realize that Prophecy speaks unto men for Edification, Exhortation, & Comfort; But a Prophet may give a Word of Correction or Warning that we may not like:
- King Hezekiah, set your house in order. *(Prophet Isaiah)*
- Prophet Agabus - Paul's belt.
- We need to learn that "Prophecy Releases The Potential Of The Purpose Of God", it is not Automatic.

Introduction

I was Born Again as a Baptist boy at 5 years of age. In my early years my father was a Baptist Pastor having come up through the ranks so to speak in the Baptist Church. He was a Deacon, a Head Deacon, a Sunday School teacher, the Superintendent of Sunday School, the Chairman of the Missions Board, all of the various positions one could hold while not being an Ordained Minister. Eventually he became a Licensed Minister and then an Ordained Minister. He became Assistant Pastor, then Associate Pastor, and finally Senior Pastor.

When I was a Freshman in High School things began to change. My Baptist Pastor father had begun to listen to Charismatic, Pentecostal and Word of Faith teachers and preachers on the radio…something Baptist Pastors did not do. Next he and my Mom went to visit a Pentecostal church, that was the night everything changed. The Pastor of that church as he was walking around preaching that night had a Word of Knowledge and stopped right next to my Dad and said: "There is a Baptist Pastor here tonight who is hungering for more of God, stand up brother." Well my Mom and Dad both stood up...but not for long as this Pastor laid hands on them they were Filled with the Holy Spirit, got slain in the Spirit and came up off the floor speaking in other Tongues.

My Father came back to his Baptist church so excited about the new experience in God that he and my Mom had and couldn't wait to tell the church all about it. Well don't you know that some folks thought Pastor had lost his mind? Some of the church followed Mom & Dad and moved into the Fullness of the Spirit and some ran thinking it was heresy. One night as my Father and I were alone at the church in what we used to call: "A Praise Gathering" the Spirit of God fell on me, and I fell on the floor. I can remember being on the floor half in the natural realm and half in the spiritual realm; and hearing my Father dancing around the church with his change jingling in his pockets exclaiming: "My son will never be the same again!"

Well, he was right! I have never been the same since that night when I was 15 years old in that little Baptist *(now Bapticostal)* church in Irvington, NJ. I came up off the floor like I was shot out of a catapult. I began to run around the church and immediately was praising God in my new heavenly tongue. It was not long after this, after reading some of the books by Rev. Kenneth E. Hagin that the Inspiration Gifts of the Holy Spirit *(Prophecy,*

Tongues, and Interpretation of Tongues) began to operate in my life.

When I started to prophesy way back then, it was 1977. I was not prophesying at the level that I prophesy at now some 45 years later. I started at a very basic elementary level that I call the "simple gift of prophecy" *(a term I borrowed from Rev. Kenneth E Hagin).* But through the years as I have matured, so has the gift in its development in my life. Around the year 2000, after operating as an Evangelist for 13 years after my graduation from Rhema Bible Training Center *(now called College)* in 1987, God began to deal with me about moving into the Prophet's office, which I greatly resisted. *(It should also be noted that I actually began teaching and preaching as a teenager around 1979 at 17 years of age.)*

Finally I came to the place, which I will get into more detail about throughout this book, where I yielded and submitted to the will of God for my life and began the process of switching *offices* or *functions*. I then went through a period of about 3-4 years of major transition and transformation until around 2003 or 2004 when I felt comfortable with my new assignment and calling. With the new function came greater levels of "Prophetic Gifting" and a desire to teach others what God had taught me.

As I sit to write this book reflecting on my years of ministry, I realize that a major focus of my teaching, training, mentoring, counseling, and question answering has dealt with the subjects included in the title of this book: **Prophets, Prophecy & Prophetic Gifting.** It is my prayer that God will use this book to shed light on where you are in your development process…That you might see yourself somewhere in the pages of this book…That you will have a greater understanding regarding all things Prophetic.

From The Beginning: Prophecy vs. Prophets

Almost every time I teach on Prophecy, Prophets, or Prophetic Gifting; I usually make this statement somewhere as a foundational truth: *"Every Prophet will Prophesy, but not everyone who Prophesies is a Prophet!"* I have posted this statement on Facebook many times through the years, and every time I do I get a slew of "Likes." There are usually quite a few comments as well stating things like: *"Too many do not understand the difference, and the difference is vast!"* *"If the Church taught it properly we would not have this confusion."*

Getting this kind of feedback lets me know, that in spite of all the excellent teaching and books that are readily available, there is still a tremendous amount of ignorance in the Body of Christ when it comes to this subject matter.

First of all, the Gift of Prophecy is one of the nine Gifts of the Holy Spirit that we find listed in 1Corinthians chapter 12, which operates as the Spirit wills. The office of the Prophet is a Ministry Gift found in Ephesians 4:11, and **THE TWO ARE NOT THE SAME**!

I know that there is a teaching out there that says: *"Well, gifts are gifts are gifts."* To me that is one of the stupidest things I have ever heard. That is like saying: *"Well, sports are sports are sports."* You don't play Football with Baseball Rules! Nobody has ever thrown a home run pass, but they have thrown a touchdown pass. The Gifts of the Spirit and Five-Fold Ministry Gifts are not the same. They have different purposes and are given different ways.

When it comes to the Gift of Prophecy, like all the other eight Gifts of the Holy Spirit the Bible is quite clear that these gifts operate as the Spirit wills (1Corinthians 12:11). So it is evident from this that the Gifts of the Spirit are Gifts that the Holy Spirit gives or administers.

When it comes to the office of the Prophet, like the other four Ascension Gifts of Christ *(or five-fold ministry gifts)*, the Bible is clear that when Jesus ascended up on high, HE gave Gifts to men (Ephesians 4:8-11). So it is evident from this that the Ascension Gifts or Five-Fold Gifts are given by the Head of the Church, the Lord Jesus Christ.

One is a Gift that is given by the Holy Spirit, and the other is a Gift that is given by Jesus. The Gifts of the Spirit are given to provide for and meet needs while the Five-Fold Ministry Gifts are given to Equip the saints.

Their purpose is not even the same. So Prophecy and a Prophet are not the same thing. Yet as we stated at the beginning: *"Every Prophet will Prophesy, but not everyone who Prophesies is a Prophet!"*

PROPHECY IS JUST ONE OF THE GIFTS OF THE HOLY Spirit that will function in the life of a Prophet, not the only one, there are others as well. We will get into this in more detail when we talk about the office of the Prophet more fully. You could say that the Prophet will have the gift of Prophecy fully developed in their life and ministry and it will flow through them at a much higher level than someone who just gives a 'Prophetic Word'.

The New Testament truth is that every Born Again, Spirit Filled Believer can and should prophesy.

> *"Pursue love, and desire spiritual gifts, but especially that you may prophesy."* **1Corinthians 14:1**

Who was First Corinthians written to? To the Church that was at Corinth (1Corinthians 1:2). Notice Paul in writing to the church admonished them to desire spiritual gifts and especially prophecy [the New American Standard Bile says *desire earnestly*]. So out of all nine gifts of the Spirit that He gives to the Church to provide for and meet needs, we are told to especially desire the Gift of Prophecy. Now if it wasn't for all believers, why would the Apostle Paul say to desire this gift above all the others?

When we consider the Ministry Gift, the office of the Prophet, it is quite different. With the Gift of Prophecy, all believers are encouraged to believe for and earnestly desire it. The office of the Prophet is for those that are hand-selected by the Head of the Church, the Lord Jesus Christ. Look at the wording in Ephesians, chapter four in relation to the Ascension Gifts:

> *"And He Himself **gave some** to be apostles, some prophets, some evangelists, and some pastors and teachers."* **Ephesians 4:11** (Emphasis Mine)

Did you happen to notice the word, **Some**? Notice it did not say He gave all...it says He gave some. This indicates to us that this Gift of the office of the Prophet as well as the other four Ministry Gifts are limited. Notice also what Paul the Apostle wrote to the church at Corinth along this line:

> *"And God has appointed these in the church: **first apostles**, **second prophets**, third teachers, after that miracles, then gifts of healings, helps, administrations, varieties of tongues. **Are all apostles? Are all prophets?** Are all teachers? Are all workers of miracles? Do all have gifts of healings? Do all speak with tongues? Do all interpret? But earnestly desire the best gifts..."* **1Corinthians 12:28-31a** (Emphasis Mine)

The way Paul is asking the questions rhetorically the obvious answer is NO! All are not Apostles! All are not Prophets! All do not have the Gifts of Healings! Did you also notice that Prophecy is not mentioned here? I believe that was not by mistake or happenstance because as we saw in the above references, all Believers could and should Prophesy.

So clearly we can see that the Gift of Prophecy is for all Believers, but the office of the Prophet is for a select few.

THE GIFT OF PROPHECY

I functioned as a Prophet for 16 years of my ministry, teaching on the Gifts of the Spirit in general, and the Gift of Prophecy specifically. Frequently I get asked: *"What exactly is Prophecy anyway?"* Prophecy is a supernatural manifestation of the Spirit where a believer is inspired to speak a message from God in a known language *(Known to the speaker)*. What do I mean by a known language and known to the speaker?

The only language that I know how to speak is English, so therefore I can only prophesy in English. I met a man on one of my trips to Africa that spoke seven languages. Guess how many languages he could prophesy in? You guessed it…seven…because he knew how to speak seven.

Inspiration is an important aspect of Prophecy which cannot be overlooked. The Bible tells us that all Scripture was given by inspiration (2Timothy 3:16). Webster's Dictionary defines inspiration as follows: *a divine influence or action on a person believed to qualify him or her to receive and communicate sacred revelation.* The original Greek carries the meaning, GOD BREATHED. So we could say that just as all Scripture was God breathed, so also every PROPHETIC WORD will also be God breathed.

Does that mean that we are putting the PROPHETIC WORD on the same level as the Canon of Scripture? **One Thousand Times NO!** The Apostle Peter wrote:

*"And this **voice which came from heaven we heard, when we were with him in the holy mount**. We have also a more sure word of prophecy; whereunto ye do well that ye take heed, as unto a light that shineth in a dark place, until the day dawn, and the day star arise in your hearts: Knowing this first that **no prophecy of the scripture** is of any private interpretation."* **2 Peter 1:18-20 KJV** (Emphasis Mine)

THEREFORE WHAT WE HOLD IN THAT BLACK LEATHER-bound book we call the Bible is the more sure Word of Prophecy that all PROPHETIC WORDS are measured against! But it is important to realize that the Prophecy of today comes the same way Scripture came to those who wrote it, by the inspiration of the Holy Spirit.

*"For prophecy never came by the will of man, but **holy men of God spoke as they were moved by the Holy Spirit**."* **2 Peter 1:21** (Emphasis Mine)

So just as holy men of God were moved by the Holy Spirit in the writing of Scripture, so Holy Men and Women of God are still being moved by the same Holy Spirit to speak and declare the 'Current Word of God.' So if there is no inspiration, there can be no true PROPHETIC WORD!

So what it is Prophecy in its simplest form? The book of Revelation tells us:

> *"And I fell at his feet to worship him. But he said to me, 'See that you do not do that! I am your fellow servant, and of your brethren who have the testimony of Jesus. Worship God! For the* **testimony of Jesus** *is the* **spirit of prophecy**.*'"* **Revelation 19:10** (Emphasis Mine)

So to make a compound definition of Prophecy, we would come up with, **speaking by the inspiration of the Spirit in a language that you know how to speak,** where you share the testimony of Jesus.

ANOTHER SCRIPTURE THAT HELPS US IMMENSELY IS FOUND in Paul's first letter to the Church at Corinth.

> *"But he that prophesieth speaketh unto men to* **edification**, *and* **exhortation**, *and* **comfort**.*"* **1 Corinthians 14:3 KJV** (Emphasis Mine)

This is what Dad Hagin (Rev. Kenneth E. Hagin) used to call the SIMPLE GIFT OF PROPHECY; a term that I have adopted from him and have been using in my teachings for over 20 years now. In this verse the Apostle Paul outlines for us three things that are accomplished by the release of the PROPHETIC WORD:

- Edification – Build you up.
- Exhortation – Charge you up.
- Comfort – Cheer you up.

Now all of as at one time or another in our Christian walk needs one or more of these three benefits of the PROPHETIC WORD in our life. The reason that this type of Prophecy is referred to as the SIMPLE GIFT OF PROPHECY is because it is extremely basic and general without revelation or specifics. This is the level of Prophecy that we all start at. When I was a 15-year-old freshman in high school and began to Prophesy, this is where I started.

These types of words are usually things like, *"The Lord is so moved by our worship today and He is wrapping His arms of love around us."* This is nothing deep or heavy, just a very encouraging and uplifting word. This is the type of WORD that would normally come out during our worship service at that time we call, 'The Holy Hush.' It would normally be delivered by (for lack of a better term, even though I really don't like the term) a lay person (not a 5-fold Minister).

This is where we all start, with WORDS along this line. We must understand that the Prophetic is just like life and going to school. When we are in school and studying Math, we don't start with Algebra and Geometry, we start with basic addition like 2 + 2 = 4. When we have basic addition down they move us to subtraction. When we get subtraction down they move us to multiplication, then division. At this point are we ready for Algebra and Geometry? Heavens No! We still haven't learned fractions, decimal points, or percentages yet.

Well, things in the Spirit in general, and specifically with the Prophetic, since it is the subject of this book, is no different. We have folks who want to start out with Prophetic Algebra because they see a seasoned, fully developed Prophet operate at a remarkably high level of the Prophetic Gift. It just doesn't work that way. If you haven't yet mastered Prophetic Addition, you will stay at that level until you do. There are levels and stages of Prophetic Gifting from the Simple Gift of Prophecy all the way up to the office of the Prophet. We will devote one chapter of this book just to that.

LET US DO A QUICK REVIEW BEFORE WE GO ANY FURTHER. Prophecy is an inspired utterance. Without inspiration there can be no legitimate PROPHETIC WORD. Prophecy is held up against the standard of the written Word of God. Prophecy in its simplest form is the Testimony of

Jesus that speaks for Edification, Exhortation and/or Comfort.

Types of Prophecy

There are four general types of prophetic words:

- Public
- Personal
- Directional
- Correctional

Out of these four types, the first two, Public and Personal are the most common. A Public Prophetic Word is that general type of word which we have discussed above that we call the Simple Gift of Prophecy. Again, this is the starting place where everybody who flows prophetically starts and then progresses from. We call it a Public Prophecy because it is spoken out publicly to the entire congregation.

The Personal Prophetic Word is also quite common but quite as common as the Public Prophetic Word. We call it the Personal Prophetic Word because it occurs when the speaker singles out a person or a specific group of persons and gives a word directly to them. While the Public Prophetic Word is given in general to the congregation, the Personal Prophetic Word is given specifically to the person or group of people (for example like a ministry team, or a Husband and Wife). In this case the word is directed solely to them, and is really not applicable to everyone else who may be present at the meeting.

I am sure that most of you have seen both of these types of Prophetic Words before if you have been around either, Charismatic, Pentecostal, Word of Faith or Apostolic & Prophetic circles. The other two types of Prophetic Words, the Directional Prophetic Word and the Correctional Prophetic Word are not nearly as common. The first one, the Directional Prophetic Word is just as it is described, it is a word that is designed to speak and give direction to your life. This type of word can be delivered as a Public Word to a congregation or as a Personal Word to an individual.

The last type of Prophetic Word, the Correctional Prophetic Word, is just as it is described, it is a word that is designed to bring correction to your life. This type of word like the Directional Prophetic Word can also be delivered as a Public Word to a congregation, or as a Personal Word to an individual. However when dealing with these last two types of Prophetic Words the Directional and Correctional, they will most of the time be delivered by very seasoned Ministry Gifts like an Apostle or a Prophet. It is not even normal (not to say that it could not happen) for even the other three Ministry Gifts: Evangelists, Pastors, and Teachers to give one of these two types of Words.

The Personal Prophetic Word will not normally be delivered by someone who is not in a Five-Fold Ministry office (Apostle, Prophet, Evangelist, Pastor and Teacher).

Again, not to say that it won't ever happen, but it would not be the normal circumstance.

So as we look at classifications of people who might prophesy, it could be considered like this:

- John Q Christian – will operate in the PUBLIC PROPHETIC WORD (Simple Gift of Prophecy).
- Someone with a RECOGNIZED PROPHETIC GIFTING (a term we have not mentioned yet but will later in more detail) – will operate in the PERSONAL PROPHETIC WORD *and* the PUBLIC PROPHETIC WORD.
- A Five-Fold Minister - will operate in the PERSONAL PROPHETIC WORD *and* the PUBLIC PROPHETIC WORD.
- An Apostle or Prophet – will operate in the CORRECTIONAL PROPHETIC WORD, the DIRECTIONAL PROPHETIC WORD, the PERSONAL PROPHETIC WORD and the PUBLIC PROPHETIC WORD.

Judging The Prophetic Word

It is particularly important that we learn how to judge the prophetic word. If you have been around as long as I have you most likely have discovered that many folks *prophe-lie* as opposed to prophesy! You may also have discovered that there are quite a few 'Granola Christians' out there, those that are fruity, flakey and nutty. We can just take every "supposed" prophetic word as being from God. The Scriptures are quite clear on this:

> *"Don't suppress the Spirit, and don't stifle those who have a word from the Master. On the other hand, **don't be gullible. Check out everything, and keep only what's good.**"* 1Thessalonians 5:19-21 MSG (Emphasis Mine)

> *"Do not quench the Spirit; do not despise prophetic utterances. But **examine everything carefully; hold fast to that which is good.**"* 1Thessalonians 5:19-21 NASB (Emphasis Mine)

Did you notice the wording in both The Message and the New American Standard which I highlighted in **bold** print? **Don't Be Gullible! Examine Everything Carefully! Check Out Everything! Hold Fast or Keep That Which Is Good!** Folks, face it, this is our responsibility. We must do this. The Apostle John said:

> *"Dear friends, **do not believe everyone who claims to speak by the Spirit. You must test them** to see if the spirit they have comes from God. **For there are many false prophets in the world.** This is how we know if they have the Spirit of God: If a person claiming to be a prophet acknowledges that Jesus Christ came in a real body, that person has the Spirit of God. But if someone claims to be a prophet and does not acknowledge the truth about Jesus, that person is not from God. Such a person has the spirit of the Antichrist, which you heard is coming into the world and indeed is already here."* 1John 4:1-3 NLT (Emphasis Mine)

LOOK AT WHAT JOHN SAID: *DO NOT BELIEVE EVERYONE WHO CLAIMS TO SPEAK BY THE SPIRIT! YOU MUST TEST THEM! THERE ARE MANY FALSE PROPHETS IN THE WORLD!* Again, it is up to us to do this. Don't just take or believe any old thing that comes down the pike that somebody says is from God. Check it out to make sure that it is from God before you receive it.

Some folks out there have learned the art of spiritual manipulation and witchcraft by using verbiage that has become accepted as a normal prophetic speech pattern. We have phrases that we use like: *"My Little Children,"* or *"Thus says The Lord,"* or *"So Says The Lord."* All these little phrases are accepted. Now we have folks who prophesy what they want you to do, and throw a few of these phrases in to lend credibility to the lies they are spewing. The unsuspecting swallow it hook, line and sinker, and are manipulated into something that some man or woman wanted them to do, **but it has nothing to do with what God wants for their life**.

This just ought not to be. If we would learn how to judge these phony bologna "supposed words," we would spare ourselves a lot of heartache, pain, wasted time and wasted motion pursuing things that God never intended us to pursue.

You may say, *"Mike, that is well and good, but how do I judge the PROPHETIC WORD?"* I am so glad you asked!

1. Does the PROPHETIC WORD line up with Scripture?

2. Does the Prophetic Word do any of the three things listed in 1Corinthians 14:3? Does it either bring Edification, Exhortation and/or Comfort?
3. Does the Prophetic Word bear witness with your recreated human spirit?
4. Does the Prophetic Word come to pass?

These are the criteria that a Prophetic Word must pass in order to be considered as being a legitimate Word that is from God. If the Word is contrary to the revealed will of God in His Holy Word, I don't care who said it. I don't care how many degrees and letters they have after their name. I don't care if they are called: Bishop, Apostle, Prophet, Overseer, Reverend, Doctor or whatever. If it is contrary to the Bible, **IT IS NOT GOD!**

Secondly, if the Prophetic Word does not do any one or combination of the three things listed in 1Corinthians 14:3, **IT IS NOT FROM GOD!** Again, I don't care who said it, I don't care how many degrees and letters they have after their name. I don't care if they are called: Bishop, Apostle, Prophet, Overseer, Reverend, Doctor or whatever. If it doesn't edify, if it doesn't exhort, if it doesn't bring comfort, or any combination thereof, **Don't Receive That Word!**

Third, if the Prophetic Word does not bear witness with your spirit, **IT IS NOT FROM GOD!** Remember that the Word tells us that the Spirit bears witness with our spirit that we are children of God (Romans 8:16). If I were to ask you if you were saved, you would just instantly say "Yes," without hesitation. Why? Because the Spirit of God is bearing witness with your spirit. You just know because you know down deep inside. Sometimes I like to say **you know in your knower.** Learn to go by what is in your knower, not by what is in your head.

I sometimes tell folks that if you want to be a success in life, cut your head off. Now of course I don't mean that literally. The Bible is clear that we should not lean on our own understanding, but in all our ways acknowledge Him (Proverbs 3:5-6). Paul also said in Romans, chapter 8 that as many as are led by the Spirit of God, they are the sons of God (Romans 8:14). If we would learn to be led by the Holy Spirit through our knower, that place that Jesus spoke of when He said out of your belly will flow rivers of living water (John 7:38), and ignore our heads, we wouldn't miss it. If the PROPHETIC WORD doesn't sit right in your spirit, **DON'T RECEIVE IT!**

BEFORE WE JUMP TO THE LAST WAY TO JUDGE THE PROPHETIC WORD, allow me to touch on something that is closely related to what we just discussed under number three. Many times when we receive a PERSONAL PROPHETIC WORD, it is something that is already in our spirit. But when the prophetic word comes, it brings confirmation to what is already in our spirit. Or it may add clarity to what is already in our spirit, or it may expand upon what is already in our spirit. That being said, if you get a prophetic word that is totally **new revelation** to you, by that I mean that it is not in your spirit at all, there will still be a witness of it in your spirit. And even though you may not understand it, because there is a witness of it, **HOLD ONTO IT!**

Lastly, we come to: Does the PROPHETIC WORD come to pass? This is the one that kind of throws a monkey wrench into things as it is not as cut and dried as the other three. Quite often I hear folks say that, "So and So prophesied XYZ to me and it didn't come to pass, so either they are a 'False Prophet,' or they missed God, that 'Word' was not from God!"

Has anyone else ever heard that? Have you ever thought that? Before we can just make these kind of generalizations, there are three things to consider:

1. Was it a CONDITIONAL PROPHETIC WORD?
2. Was there a timeframe given in the prophetic word, or do you have God's Timing?
3. What are you doing with the prophetic word'?

Now I can hear some of you asking, *"What on earth is a Conditional Prophetic Word?* You may be thinking, *"I thought when something was prophesied it was an automatic thing."* Well since we compare all prophetic words to the Scriptures; let us see if that thought process holds water. We will look at two familiar passages of Scripture.

> *"If you are **willing and obedient**, You shall eat the good of the land."* **Isaiah 1:19** (Emphasis Mine)

In this verse of Scripture we find a promise that states that you will eat the good of the land. However, we also find two conditions which must be met before we can expect to walk in the promise of eating the good of the land. The two conditions that must be met are that we be **willing and obedient**. Well, what happens if we are not willing and obedient? Then we have no right to the promise of eating the good of the land. Nor will we.

Notice it is not enough to be willing or obedient; we must be willing *and* obedient. It is very much like the story of the parent who tells their six-year-old son to go to bed. The child replies: *"I don't want to go to bed."* To which the parent replies: *"I said go to bed!"* To which the child replies: *"I don't want to go to bed!"* Now the parent, a little angry, proceeds towards the child raising their hand and their voice speaking through clenched teeth saying: *"I SAID GO TO BED!"*

At this point the child knows a beating is about to come. So reluctantly the child goes to bed so as to avoid the wrath of their parent. Now here are the questions for this scenario: Was the child obedient? The answer would be Yes. Was the child willing? The answer would be No.

THIS IS VERY MUCH THE WAY IT IS WITH US AND GOD. In order to walk in this promise of eating the good of the land, reluctant obedience will not get the job done. It will require **both** a willing heart and the obedience. Now let us look at another familiar Scripture:

> *"Therefore* **submit to God. Resist the devil** *and he will flee from you.* **Draw near to God** *and He will draw near to you."* **James 4:7 & 8a** (Emphasis Mine)

In this verse and a half of Scripture we find two promises:

1. The devil will flee from us.
2. God will draw near to us.

These are marvelous promises that God has given us. Let us consider the first promise, that **the devil will flee from us**. My question to you is this: *Will the devil just flee from us without anything being done on our part?*

The obvious answer as we look at this Scripture is, No. The sad part is most times when folks quote this verse, they don't quote it correctly. So folks don't believe it correctly, and therefore they do not walk in the promise and usually are left wondering why it is not working.

Do you realize that when we misquote Scripture, it is not God's fault when it does not work? Tell me how many times you have heard this verse quoted like this? *"Just resist the devil and he will flee from you?"* Come on now be honest...how many times? I dare say most of the time when you hear it quoted...that is the way it is quoted.

Do you realize that is NOT what the verse says? What happened to the first condition that is mentioned? What happened to the: *"Therefore submit to God?"* Folks, if you haven't submitted first to God and to God-ordained authority, you can forget about resisting the devil> He is going to flatten you like a steamroller paving fresh black top. You may ask, *"Why Mike?"* Because you haven't met the condition of submitting to God first. You first submit to God and God-ordained authority, then you resist the devil, then he will flee from you.

The second promise we see in this text is that God will draw near to us. Again, I ask: *"Will God just draw near to us without any action on our part?"* Again, the obvious answer is, No. The verse says to draw near to God, than God will draw near to us. What happens if we don't draw near to God? Then God will not draw near to us. Can you see how these promises that are in these verses are conditional, predicated on the fact that we do something, then God will do something? Have you ever noticed how often in Scripture it seems that God speaks in this manner: *"If you will do this, then I will do this?"* *"If you do this, then this will happen?"* If God speaks that way in His written word, doesn't it stand to reason that He would speak that way in the PROPHETIC WORD?

SO MANY TIMES IF YOU EXAMINE THE WORDING OF THE PROPHETIC WORD you will notice similar speech patterns. I remember once I gave someone a prophetic word that stated: *"As you continue in this path...then XYZ."* Now what happens if that person does not continue in that path? What happens if they veer off course? Then XYZ is not going to happen. But you may be thinking the PROPHETIC

Word said XYZ was going to happen. Well that is a half-truth, and a half-truth is a lie. What the Prophetic Word said was: *"As you continue in this path..."*

Now this individual could have not stayed the course, changed direction, and robbed themselves of what God was promising them. The choice was theirs to obey the instruction in the Prophetic Word in order to walk in the promise of the 'Prophetic Word. If they didn't obey the instruction and not inherit the promise, was that my fault as the Prophet who gave the Prophetic Word?

No, no more than it is God's fault when we don't submit to Him so we can resist the devil, so that he would flee from us. Can you see how the Prophetic Word works just like the written Word?

So when we examine does the Prophetic Word come to pass we must ask ourselves: *"Was it a Conditional Prophetic Word"?* So often we don't understand the language of the Prophetic! The language of the Prophetic, even though it comes out with the speech patterns and personality of the vessel that is delivering it, is just like Scripture in that each of the writer's had their own personality and speech patterns come out in their writings too. Just look at Peter and Paul, their writing styles were certainly different, just as individuals who Prophesy will have different styles, yet the element will remain the same many times you will still hear if you will ABC than I will XYZ, when you do that is a Conditional Prophetic Word not an Absolute Prophetic Word.

The second thing to consider in does the PROPHETIC WORD come to pass is timing. Either was there a timing given or do you know God's timing for the PROPHETIC WORD? So often when we get a 'Word' we are ready to just run off with that 'Word' ready to do whatever we can to implement that 'Word' and make it happen right now. I know from first-hand experience that this can be an accident going somewhere to happen.

AS I LOOK BACK OVER MY LIFE I CAN LOOK AT MANY prophetic words that I received that took years to even begin to come to pass, and some I am still waiting for. Don't get in a hurry trying to make what God told you come to pass! Let us look at this familiar portion of Scripture as a foundation to draw from and refer to in order to help us understand God's timing:

> *"Then the Lord answered me and said: 'Write the vision And make it plain on tablets, That he may run who reads it. For the vision is yet for an **appointed time**; But at the end it will speak, and it will not lie. Though it tarries, **wait for it**; Because it will surely come, It will not tarry.'"* **Habakkuk 2: 2 & 3** (Emphasis Mine)

I remember in 1982, right after I got married, my wife and I were on our way to Tulsa, Oklahomalahoma for me to attend Rhema Bible Training Center (now Rhema Bible Training College). We made a slight detour on our way from New Jersey to Oklahoma via Michigan, where my sister Bonnie and her family lived at the time for a visit.

During that visit we went to church with them and her Pastor, Robert Doorn (known to many the world over as Papa Doorn) called me out and prophesied to me on the Sunday night we were there. Here is an excerpt of what he prophesied to me that night, August 29, 1982:

> *"The Lord would say to you tonight Brother Mike, The Spirit of God would say, that while your Mother and Father are going to the mission field, they're only going to blaze a trail before you. For surely, the trail they will blaze, shall even be a trail that you yourself will walk and minister under the anointing of My Spirit. You shall see multitudes healed and delivered and set free by My power, for behold, I'll put the Word of Faith within you..."*

Now here is what we need to learn about the Prophetic. **THERE IS TIMING TO THE PROPHETIC!** I didn't take my first missionary trip to Africa until 1987, right after I graduated from Rhema, five years later. I didn't really see multitudes get healed through my ministry until 1993 on a short-term missionary trip to Uganda during a crusade where the Gift of Faith fell on me, six years after my first missionary trip, and 11 years after I received the Prophetic Word.

The true legitimate prophetic word of God will always come to pass, but not on our time, on God's time, and more times than not, they are not the same! What I think we fail to realize is that the language of the Prophetic can confuse us. For example, many times in prophetic words we will hear God say, *"Soon."* Well, we immediately run off trying in our strength and ability to cause that word to come to pass because God said, *"Soon."*

We must remember that "Soon" to God and "Soon" to us mean two different things. God lives outside of time, and we live in time. God measures time totally different than we do. Peter gives us a clue:

> *"But do not let this **one fact** escape your notice, beloved, that with the Lord **one day is like a thousand years, and a thousand years like one day.**"* **2 Peter 3:8 NASB** (Emphasis Mine)

So if we take this formula that Peter gives and apply it to Bible Prophecy it helps us in interpreting the Scriptures.

> *"He will revive us after **two days**; He will raise us up on the **third day** that we may live before Him. So let us know, let us press on to know the Lord. His going forth is certain as the dawn; and He will come to us like the rain, like the spring rain watering the earth."* **Hosea 6:2 & 3 NASB** (Emphasis Mine)

I want you to pay attention to the highlighted words in this text: **two days** & **third day**. In this portion of Scripture the Prophet is declaring that some things will take place after two days *and* on the third day. My question to you is this: Was this Scripture fulfilled after two days from when it was written?

Most of you who understand where we are in God's timetable understand that these promises that the Prophet declared are things that we are walking in today. Using Peter's time calculation formula, it has been two days, or 2000 years since Christ was here, and we are now in the beginning of the third day, or the third 1000-year period. *(I have a whole message I preach from this text titled: "Where Are We Now," but that is not the focus of this section of this book, understanding God's timing is.)*

If God has given you a promise…it will come to pass! Just don't be in a hurry trying to make it come to pass. There is Timing to every Prophetic Word. Remember it is for an **appointed time**. Though it tarries…WAIT for it…for it will surely come!

I WOULD LIKE TO GIVE YOU ANOTHER EXAMPLE FROM MY life which I believe will help you. This time the revelation that I received from the Lord came through a different manifestation of the Spirit, and one that many folks in the Church don't walk in or even understand. One time recently when I recounted this story in a sermon as an illustration, I had some folks looking at me like I had three heads or something because it was so far out of their understanding. Let us again look at the Word of God to lay the foundation:

> *"Therefore let him who **speaks in a tongue pray that he may interpret**. For if **I pray in a tongue**, my*

spirit prays, but my understanding is unfruitful." **1Corinthians 14: 13-14** (Emphasis Mine)

There are two applications that can be made from these two verses. They are similar, yet different. They both deal with TONGUES, but one deals with the PUBLIC GIFT OF TONGUES which must be interpreted to be in order Biblically, the other deals with your Prayer Language, which doesn't need to be interpreted, but it is to your benefit if it is.

Let us consider the first one regarding the public Gift of Tongues. Notice the Apostle Paul said if you speak in a tongue, pray that you may interpret. That is because the Public Gift MUST ALWAYS be interpreted. We know this because later in this chapter Paul gives this direction:

> *"If **anyone speaks in a tongue**, let there be two or at the most three, each in turn, and let one interpret. But **if there is no interpreter, let him keep silent in church**, and let him speak to himself and to God."* **1Corinthians 14: 27 & 28** (Emphasis Mine)

There are many things I could bring out of this passage, but we are not teaching on Tongues here, so I will limit my observations and explanations to the matter at hand. Paul is basically saying that if you speak in tongues but there is no one to **interpret the Public Message,** don't speak out the Public Message. A MIKE RULE…

not a Bible Rule is: *"If you can't give the interpretation, don't give the message!"*

Let us now go back to 1Corinthians 14:13-14 to make our application regarding your Prayer Language. Paul says that when you pray in Tongues, your spirit prays but your understanding or mind is unfruitful, or does not understand. However, before he says that, he says if you speak in a tongue, pray that you may ***interpret***. Why should your mind or understanding be unfruitful or not understand when you pray in Tongues? **Ask God to give you the Interpretation of what you prayed in your Prayer Language (Tongues).**

ONE TIME SOMEBODY ASKED DR. ORAL ROBERTS WHAT the secret to his success in the ministry was. How many think Oral Roberts had some success in the ministry? Are you ready for his secret to success? He said: *"I pray in other Tongues to God, then I ask Him for the Interpretation to what I prayed, then I pray out the Interpretation in English what I prayed in Tongues, then I go and do the Interpretation."*

So how does this relate to us? We can pray in our Prayer Language, which is always praying God's will, then pray back the Interpretation of what we prayed in Tongues, and we have just prayed back to ourselves the Will of God regarding our lives, or the situation we were praying over in our Prayer Language. We now have God's direction.

Now to how this worked in my life and how I got direction and almost missed God by not understanding timing: Right after I graduated from Rhema in 1987, I locked myself in the spare bedroom of our two-bedroom apartment in Tulsa, Oklahoma, intent on getting alone with God and getting direction for my life now that I had graduated. I was prepared to be in there for days if need be. I told my wife not to come in and get me, but to just leave me be.

I began to pray in my Prayer Language, which is how I do most of my private praying. After a while I hit a vein. I am not sure you know what I mean by hit a vein, but that is a place in the Spirit where all of a sudden it is like you have tapped into a stream or a river and just take off and go with it. As I hit this vein, I just went with it and prayed in the Spirit for quite a while with great ease. After about an hour, I began to pray back in English what I had been praying in the Spirit.

There were two major themes to my prayer that afternoon. One is not relevant to this illustration, but was extremely important for what was transpiring in the Church in 1987. If you remember, 1987 was when we had the Jim Bakker (PTL) and Jimmy Swaggart scandals, not our brightest hour. Part of the interpretation that I prayed out first that afternoon was for the restoration of both of those men of God; then came the interpretation that was for me second.

You see when I graduated I did not know what I was going to do or where I was going to go. I didn't know what the will of God was for my life. Should I stay in Oklahoma? Should I move back to New Jersey? Did God want me to go somewhere else? All I knew was I had completed my last instruction which was to finish Rhema, and graduate. Now what? So as I prayed out the second theme of that vein I hit in English I began to pray my future. I was praying about moving back to New Jersey fromOklahomato work in the ministry with my parents.

Now I knew the plan of God for my life. What I didn't know was the timing of God. This is where we can really get messed up. I tried two or three times to move back to New Jersey and make it happen in my own ability and in my own strength because I knew that God wanted me to come back to New Jersey and work with my parents. But I every time I tried it was like I hit a brick wall, and nothing fell into place or came together at all.

It took five years for that direction that I received in prayer to become a reality. And when it was time to come back everything fell into place quite quickly and easily. Within a matter of a couple of months we were back in NJ. I look back in retrospect now and realize that there were things that I needed as part of my Ministry Training that I had not yet received. There were many things that I received from my Mom and Dad growing up. There was a tremendous impartation that was received at Rhema, even though I am only now realizing the impact of the Prophetic Mantle that was imparted through Dad Hagin as I started as an Evangelist and did not really use it.

During the five years between graduating from Rhema and moving back to New Jersey I worked with Pastor Billy Joe Daugherty at Victory Christian Center. This is where the other impartations that I needed came from. I wore many hats and worked in many areas of the ministry including being one of the head ushers in the church, which allowed me to work hand-in-hand with some of God's Generals up close and personal. I also had tremendous impartations from Pastor Billy Joe who was without a doubt one of the meekest, gentlest men I have ever had the privilege to know. I needed an impartation of his spirit to soften my bull in a china shop ways.

So you see, that day when I prayed and got the direction, the direction I received was correct, but my understanding of God's timing wasn't. I thought because I had graduated from Rhema my training was complete, but God knew otherwise! He knew where to send me to get what I needed to complete my training in Oklahoma before I could move back to New Jersey.

THE THIRD THING TO CONSIDER IN DOES THE PROPHETIC WORD come to pass is what are you doing with it? This might seem like a strange question to some, but let me explain. So many times we receive a Prophetic Word and then just sit back and wait for it to manifest, but don't do anything with it. This is clearly against the admonition of the Apostle Paul to his son in the faith, the Apostle in training, Timothy.

> *"This charge I commit to you, son Timothy, according to the* **prophecies previously made concerning you, that by them you may wage the good warfare.*"***
> **1 Timothy 1:18** (Emphasis Mine)

I want you to notice what Paul said to Timothy. He was referring to Prophecies that Timothy had already (past tense) received; and that by those prophecies he could wage a good warfare. Did you ever think that you could war with your prophetic words? This is what Paul admonished Timothy to do.

I explain it to folks this way. Back in the heyday of the Word of Faith movement, there was a big push to confess the promises of the Word of God. We were taught to: "Pray the Promise, not the Problem!" If you were sick, you would find as many Scriptures as you could on physical healing in the Bible and then pray those Scriptures over your life. What were we doing? We were waging warfare with the written Word of God.

The truth is we can and should do exactly the same thing with our Prophetic Words. Paul told Timothy to wage a good warfare with them. How do we do that? First, we have to record them some way or other. Whether it is by some sort of sound recording, shorthand, long hand, whatever…but we need to have a record of them so we can refer to them and wage warfare with them. I suggest that every church and ministry get in the habit of recording Prophetic Word. Once it is recorded it can always be transcribed, which we also do quite regularly.

You may ask why should we record and transcribe prophetic words? There are two reasons:

1. So that they can be judged accurately.
2. So you will have a clear record of what was said to use in your warfare. Once you have accurate record of your PROPHETIC WORD (s) and they have been judged as being accurate, you are ready to proceed to the warfare stage.

Exactly what we used to do with the written Word of God in the Word of Faith days is what we do with our PROPHETIC WORDS. We remind God, the devil and ourselves of what God has said! The same as you would pray according to Matthew 8:17; *"Father your word says the He Himself took our infirmities and bore our sicknesses, so if He took them I don't have to have them!"* Well, you do the same thing with your PROPHETIC WORD. You say, *"Father, your Prophetic Word to me declared… (Whatever it was) …and based on your Prophetic Word to me I thank you that I walk in it, and it shall be fulfilled in my life!"*

We have to come to the place that we realize that there is just as much creative power in the LEGITIMATE PROPHETIC WORD (one that has been judged and passes the criteria) as there was in the word released in Genesis, chapter one where it records over and over again through the story of creation: *"And God said!"* Every time God said, whatever He said came to pass. And God said, "Let there be light…and light was! There is creative power released in the word of God.

The book of Hebrews puts it this way:

> *"By faith we understand that **the worlds were framed by the word of God**, so that the things which are seen were not made of things which are visible."* **Hebrews 11:3** (Emphasis Mine)

Folks, the worlds themselves were framed by the Word of God. Whatever God said is what came to be. When God speaks over your life about your purpose and destiny, He is literally framing your future, and He is waiting for you to come into agreement with Him and declare out of your mouth back to Him that which He has already declared. This is warring with your PROPHETIC WORD.

Don't you remember this verse?

> *"Put **Me in remembrance**; Let us contend together; State your case, that you may be acquitted."* **Isaiah 43:26** (Emphasis Mine)

God is telling us to remind Him of what He said. Not because He has a bad memory and does not remember, but because He wants us to come into covenant agreement with Him over what He has declared to be. He said for us to contend together, the New American Standard Bible words it this way: *"Put Me in remembrance, let us argue our case together; State your cause, that you may be proved right."* Did you see that? He said for us to argue our case together. God wants us to say, "Father you said!" It is time we learn to do that with our PROPHETIC WORDS.

Second, you are also reminding yourself of what God promised you when you rehearse your PROPHETIC WORDS. It is easy to forget what God has spoken to you. As you rehearse them, your faith gets built up and you get encouraged. Remember:

> *"So then faith comes by hearing, and hearing by the word of God."* **Romans 10:17 NKJV**

Faith comes by hearing God's word, which can be the PROPHETIC WORD just as much as it can be the written word. As you are declaring the PROPHETIC WORD, your faith is growing over what God has promised you, enabling you to believe what God has said.

Third, you are reminding the devil of what God has said. The enemy of your soul doesn't want you believing in your PROPHETIC WORD. He tries to discourage you from walking in it by telling you it will never come to pass or that God will do it for somebody else, but He will never do it for you. When you declare your PROPHETIC WORD, in essence you are saying, *"Back off, Mr. Devil, this is where I am going and this what God and I are doing!"*

You can't be passive with your PROPHETIC WORDS. You must be militant with them. You can't just sit back doing nothing, just-a-hoping-and-a-waiting for them to manifest. No! You must war with them! Remember Jesus declared:

> *"And from the days of John the Baptist until now the* **kingdom of heaven suffers violence, and the**

violent take it by force." **Matthew 11:12** (Emphasis Mine)

So before you run off and say my prophetic word did not come to pass, ask yourself, what have I done with it? It is time you stopped being relaxed with your PROPHETIC WORDS and started to be aggressive, yes, and even violent with them, and wage a good warfare with them so that they begin to come to pass.

Beginning To Flow In Prophecy

Since I am a Prophet who teaches on the Gifts of the Spirit in general and the Gift of Prophecy specifically, quite regularly I get asked questions along this line: *How do I begin to flow in the Gift of Prophecy? How do I know if it is God or just me? What if I don't sound like others that I hear prophesying?*

I want to deal with that last question first. You should not sound like someone else; you should sound like you. God created you to be a unique individual, not a "cookie cutter Christian." God desires to speak through you using your personality, speech patterns, and everyday verbiage. So often folks think they have to sound like the King James Bible when they are prophesying. Nothing could be further from the truth. If you don't speak in King James English in your normal conversations, neither should you should speak like it when you prophesy.

You must also establish as a fact that it is God's will for every Born Again, Spirit-filled Believer to prophesy!

> *"Pursue love, and* ***desire spiritual gifts****, but **especially that you may prophesy.**" **1Corinthians 14:1** (Emphasis Mine)

The Scripture is clear that we should desire Spiritual Gifts, but especially the Gift of Prophecy. If all Believers could not prophesy why would the Apostle Paul admonish us all to desire especially that we might prophesy?

> "For **you can all prophesy one by one**, that all may learn, and all may be encouraged." **1Corinthians 14:31** (Emphasis Mine)

Notice in this second verse the Apostle Paul makes it very clear…YOU CAN ALL PROPHESY! The last time I checked the word ALL meant ALL. In fact Webster's Dictionary defines the word *ALL* as:

- the whole amount, quantity, or extent of.
- as much as possible.
- every member or individual component of.
- the whole number or sum of.

Does that sound to you like anybody is excluded from being able to operate in this Gift? You need to believe for it. Desire not just the Gifts in general, but especially this one.

Now we must address something that really hinders many precious folks when they are starting out. Even though we teach and tell them to just be themselves, that God wants to use them just as they are, they still have a tendency to compare themselves to others who they see operating in the Gift of Prophecy who has been doing it much longer and is most likely at a different level and higher stage of development of the Gift.

Remember in the Introduction of this book I spoke of the fact that I started to Prophesy at 15 years of age as a Freshman in High School. Well the level that I operated at then is not the level that I operate at now some 37 years later. (We will get more into Levels of Prophetic Gifting in another chapter)

It is important to remember that when you start you will speak very general and basic words just like I did all those years ago. Everyone starts at that level. So avoid the comparison trap and NEVER GET STUCK COMPARING YOURSELF TO SOMEONE MORE EXPERIENCED THAN YOU!

Some General Rules Of Thumb

I want to give you some bullet points as general practices. These are by no means hard and fast rules, but rather more times than not it is the way things usually work within the confines of the local church service. Please bear in mind that there can be exceptions anytime the

Spirit of God chooses to do so, but normally if it does deviate from these basic general practices it will be by someone with a more advanced level or development of the Gift than the Believer just starting out. If you are just starting out, more times than not this will be the case:

- Normally prophecy will come during the praise and worship part of the service.
- There will be some sort of pause that will be a spontaneous happening led of the Spirit, not something that was planned.
- You should you wait for that pause to speak, or go to the one in authority at that time in the meeting: Pastor, Worship Leader, Guest Speaker, etc.

Two Major Streams Of The Prophetic

When it comes to understanding how the Prophetic comes to us, it will usually come one of two ways:

- The Nabi Anointing
- The Seer Anointing

The Nabi Anointing is when the words bubble up out of your spirit...the same place that Jesus spoke of when He said out of your belly will flow rivers of living water. The Seer Anointing is more visual and you either see words, pictures, or mini movies.

Quite often in the Old Testament when the Prophets spoke, the Scriptures record them saying: *"The word of the Lord came unto me saying…"*. This is the Nabi anointing and the way I minister about 75% of the time. Quite often when I prophesy I will say: *"I hear the Spirit of the Lord saying…"*. Same idea, the Nabi anointing.

THE OLD TESTAMENT ALSO TELLS US THAT A PROPHET was formerly called a Seer (1 Samuel 9:9. The reason they were called the Seer was because they could see. I only operate this way about 25% of the time. Some people like me are stronger in one than they are the other. Some only operate in one or the other. And some flow in both equally, but that is quite rare.

For the Nabi person: You will hear the first sentence or phrase of the prophecy, then you must speak that in faith and believe that God will give you the rest of it as you step out. Since I operate more by the Nabi anointing, I have much more experience to draw from to give real life illustrations.

I have a story I would like to share with you from somewhere around the year 2000, when I was beginning my transition from the office of Evangelist to the office of Prophet. One Sunday morning at a service in the church I was an Elder in at that time, God began to give me a WORD for the guest music minister who was with us that day.

All the Lord gave me was the first sentence or two. I went to the Pastor of the church and told him that I had a WORD for that guest minister. He informed me that he was getting ready to do a prayer line and asked me to hold the WORD until after he and the guest minister were done with the prayer line, and then he would give me the microphone and at that time I could give the WORD to the guest minister.

So I held onto the WORD for about ten minutes, until the prayer line was done. At that time the Pastor gave me the microphone and told the guest minister that I had a WORD for him. At this point I began to prophesy to this minister and prophesied to him for maybe five to ten minutes.

When I was done giving him the WORD, the guest minister acknowledged the WORD as being from God, and totally accurate. He declared that the Lord had been dealing with him about everything that I said. He publicly received the WORD as being from God.

When service was over that day, I became the target of the old "twenty questions" game. Everyone saw me go to the Pastor and tell him I had a WORD . They all saw me hold the WORD . Then they saw me deliver a five to ten minute WORD. What everyone wanted to know was: *"How did you get a five to ten minute WORD and hold it for ten minutes during the prayer line? How did you remember it all?"*

I blew their minds when I told them I didn't. I told them that I only had the first sentence or two and held onto that. When it was time to deliver the WORD , I just started with that and the rest just flowed out of my spirit.

Now I was at a different level in the developing of my Prophetic Gifting at this point in my life than folks would be when just starting out, but not yet at the level that I am at now. However, the principle of how it works is the same. I held onto a sentence or two, and then the rest came out. When you are first starting out you will hear a couple of words or a phrase. Step out with those couple of words or that phrase and the rest will come out by the inspiration of the Spirit. And if all you get is those couple of words or that phrase...just deliver them.

For the Seer person: You will actually see the words to the first phrase almost like the ticker tape that goes around the Times News Building in New York City's Times Square. Sometimes the Seer person will see a picture or a mini-movie.

At this point what the Seer anointed person declares is exactly what they see, whether words or pictures. Be as accurate in your description as you can be. Remember the old expression: *"A picture is worth a thousand words"*? Sometimes it might take a lot of words to describe what you see...but in the beginning just give what you see... don't try to decipher what it means...that will come later as you develop in your gift.

Is It God Or Is It Me?

Now that we understand what basic prophecy or *The Simple Gift Of Prophecy* is, and we understand the two general ways that prophecy comes to us, how do we know if it is God or us?

Again let me reiterate that you should never compare yourself to others as it will leave you feeling inadequate and afraid to step out. Whichever way it comes to you, Seer or Nabi, ask yourself: *"Does this agree with Scripture?"*

Second look to your spirit man, your innermost being, that place again that Jesus spoke of when He said out of your innermost being or out of your belly *(depending on the translation)*, and see if you have peace inside. Does it feel like velvet? Or does it feel like sandpaper?

> **Velvet = God! Sandpaper = Not God.**

I know when I first started all those years ago I would play the vacillation game, saying, *"Lord is this me or is this You?"* Many have felt that way and I am sure you will too. Quite often in the beginning, God in His mercy gives us some physical manifestations to help confirm to us that it is indeed Him. You might feel like butterflies are in your stomach, a tingling in your arms, or heat in your hands or in your belly. All are quite common.

> It should be noted that these physical manifestations do not last forever, as God expects you to grow and develop in your gifting and not require them.

When you feel these types of things, you have peace like velvet in your spirit, and you know it agrees with the Word of God, follow the protocol of your local church *(key point I can't go into here)* and go ahead and release what you believe you have. Will you start perfect? Probably not, nobody does, but we all grow. It is up to local leadership to then coach and lovingly correct you.

Not long ago we had a service where a few actually stepped out and released what was in their spirit for the first time. I went around the room and asked folks what is stirring in your belly? What feels like butterflies in your belly? I then instructed them to go ahead and release those things.

IT DOES NOT HAVE TO BE A LONG-DETAILED WORD TO BE FROM GOD! Start where you are. Remember the Word says:

> *"Having then gifts differing according to the grace that is given to us, let us use them:* **if prophecy let us prophesy in proportion to our faith.***"* **Romans 12: 6 NKJV**

You can only prophesy according to the proportion of your faith, and in the beginning your faith is not that great in this area. So again, don't compare yourself to others that are more advanced in their gifting than you are in yours.

Finally, remember that God created you as a unique, one-of-a-kind individual with your own gifts, talents, abilities, and anointing on your life. Nobody else is like you. You were created to be an original, not a copy. Be yourself! Don't try to sound like somebody else!

Sound like you! God will use your normal every day speech patterns, verbiage and conversation style just as much as He will use anybody else's. You don't have to be somebody you are not to be used by God in the Gift of Prophecy!

Following Protocol

Following protocol is an area that many don't think about when it comes to the Prophetic, yet it is one of the most important things that there is. Let's begin with some Scripture to lay a foundation.

> "For **God is not the author of confusion** but of peace, as in all the churches of the saints…Therefore, brethren, desire earnestly to prophesy, and do not forbid to speak with tongues. **Let all things be done decently and in order.**" **1Corinthians 14: 33, 39 & 40** (Emphasis Mine)

In this fairly well-known text the Apostle Paul is giving instructions for the operation of the Gifts of the Holy Spirit in the local church. I want you to notice that he said that God is not the author of confusion. I have seen many things in the church over the last 40+ years since I first was filled with the Holy Spirit and began to operate in the Simple Gift of Prophecy. Some good and some bad. It is sad to see confusion about the operation of these things, and it ought not to be. When we do see this, realize that God is not in it.

I have heard many people say, *"Well you know I could not help it. The Holy Spirit moved me."* Well if there is confusion as a result of your actions, I must say He did not, because this text clearly says that **God is not the author of confusion.** I sometimes say in jest, but not really: *"I don't doubt that it was a spirit, but it wasn't the Holy Spirit!"*

Protocol Defined

Webster's Dictionary defines protocol as follows:

- A system of rules that explain the correct conduct and procedures to be followed in formal situations.
- A code prescribing strict adherence to correct etiquette and precedence.

So when we talk about protocol within the local church we are talking about the rules of correct conduct, or the correct etiquette within that particular local church. Every local church has their own rules, procedures, and etiquette regarding how things are done in that house. The protocol is set by the leadership of that local house.

It is important that we learn and adhere to the protocol of the house we happen to be in at any given time. To operate outside of the protocol would be out of order.

We would be guilty of violating what Paul declared should be our conduct with everything being done decently and in order. Protocol is not designed to keep people from flowing and manifesting the Gifts of the Spirit, but rather to help make sure we keep in line with the Scriptural precedent of everything being done in an orderly manner. (1Corinthians 14:40 NASB)

General Rules

There are some rules that are laid out in Scripture that would be applicable in every house. The first general rule is that all can prophesy.

> *"For **you can all prophesy** one by one, that all may learn, and all may be encouraged."* **1Corinthians 14:31** (Emphasis Mine)

The Apostle Paul makes it quite plain that all can prophesy. The second general rule is that we can only prophesy one at a time and it is in the same Scripture.

> *"For you can all prophesy **one by one**, that all may learn, and all may be encouraged."* **1Corinthians 14:31** (Emphasis Mine)

Here we see that the Apostle Paul clearly states one by one, meaning each one in his or her turn.

Specific Rules

In my years in the church I have encountered several different types of protocol in local churches, but generally they boil down to four major types.

The first type is what I call the "OPEN SEASON" or "POPCORN PROPHECY." In this type of church not only is anyone and everyone permitted to prophesy at will, but they can just pop up and speak out in the congregation as long as it is quiet and nobody else is speaking. Generally this type of protocol works best in a home home-meeting or home-fellowship.

The second type I call the "SCREENING PROCESS." This is one of the most popular protocols that we see in the church today. The person with the WORD is encouraged to come forward and share the general gist of the WORD with a screener assigned by the leadership, who will judge the WORD before it is given the green light to be released to the body. This will allow the WORD to be amplified and possibly recorded.

The third type I call the "MODIFIED SCREENING PROCESS." It is quite similar to the second type with one caveat *[this is where the Scripture that says - know those that labor among you really comes into play]*, because the person coming forward with the WORD is already known in the house for having a good track record and reputation. Because of this, they are not asked for a gist of the WORD, they are just given the mic to release their WORD.

The fourth type I call, "DON'T CALL US, WE'LL CALL YOU." In this protocol, which is the most controlling type, the leadership only allows people to bring forth WORDS after the leadership calls on someone. In this type of protocol one is not permitted to go to leadership suggesting that they have something. It is an accepted reality that if God gives someone in the congregation something, God will speak to leadership and let them know that said individual has received something from the Lord.

KNOW WHERE YOU ARE

It is so vital that you know the protocol of the house you are in. Suppose you are a member of a church that operates in type one that I called "OPEN SEASON." You are just used to popping up in the midst of the congregation in a service and speaking out, *"Thus Saith The Lord...."* Now you happen to be visiting a church that practices type number two, "THE SCREENING PROCESS."

If you just pop up like you normally do in your home church, which is the first protocol, you are now out of order in type two because you are violating their protocol. Can you see that? One of the best and easiest keys to following protocol in any house is to practice a game we all used to play as kids – "Follow The Leader." If you follow what the leadership is doing, you will never violate the protocol of the house and be out of order.

I remember several years ago when I was going through my transition from Evangelist to Prophet, God had me in a church for a season. It was my third time visiting that church, and God gave me a Word for that house. I didn't know anybody in that house yet, it was only my third time there. Not only that, but I had not seen anyone prophesy in the house yet, although I knew they believed in the operation of the Gifts.

As I was there wrestling with God as to how to go about releasing what I felt like He was giving me for that house or even if I should, two things happened. *(Anybody ever wrestle and argue with God before like this besides me?)* The first thing that happened was the worship leader began to sing the Mercy Me song: *Word of God Speak.* At this point I said, *"Okay Lord, I get it, but how do I release it?"*

You see even though I didn't know what their protocol was, God did! He said to me, *"Go over to that youth Pastor and tell him what you have."* So I was obedient to what the Lord told me. I went and told the youth Pastor. The youth Pastor then walked up to the platform and called over the Pastor and was speaking into his ear. The next thing I know the Pastor is calling me up to the platform. I then tell him what I have. He says to stay there, and as soon as the worship leader is finished with the song they are currently singing, he will give me the microphone and he wants me to give the Word.

So I discovered that this church was a type-two church, and the rest of the season that I was there I operated in the confines of that protocol because that was how they operated. If you are not sure if the church is a type one, two, three, or four; ask God. He knows, and will gladly tell you because He wants you to operate within the confines the protocol of that house and not be out of order. Always adapt yourself and how you operate to where you are.

Submission & Authority

The last aspect to operating in protocol is to understand submission and authority. The principle is this: If you are not under authority, you can't exercise authority. This is an important Kingdom Principle, and it holds in many areas of Kingdom life, not just observing protocol. The Roman Centurion who came to Jesus on behalf of his sick servant is a great example of this.

> *"But the officer said, 'Lord, I am not worthy to have you come into my home. Just say the word from where you are, and my servant will be healed. I know this because* **I am under the authority of my superior officers, and I have authority over my soldiers.** *I only need to say, Go, and they go, or Come, and they come. And if I say to my slaves, Do this, they do it.'"* **Matthew 8:8 & 9 NLT** (Emphasis Mine)

Notice the Centurion said that he was under the authority of his superior officers, and that he had authority over his soldiers. Because he was under authority, he could then exercise authority. We can only exercise authority to the degree that we are under authority!

It is so vital that we learn this. We can't afford anymore renegades or Lone Rangers running around the church who are not submitted to or accountable to anybody, and then expect that they should just be able to prophesy and speak into people's lives. No Way! If you are not under authority, you can't exercise authority! **You are operating outside of Biblical protocol.**

Please allow me to illustrate this point by recounting a story from my experience back in the mid-90s. Back at that time I was still functioning as an Evangelist. It was a few years before I transitioned to the function of a Prophet. I was functioning as an Elder and Director of adult education at a local church in Rahway, New Jersey. While there, they did not have a head usher, so I was also functioning as an interim head usher, as I had that in my experience from when I lived in Tulsa, Oklahoma during the late 80s.

After I graduated from Rhema Bible Training Center, (now Rhema Bible Training College) in 1987, I worked in multiple areas of helps ministry at Victory Christian Center, where Billy Joe Daugherty was the Senior Pastor. One of the areas I served in was as head usher of the 11:00 AM Sunday Morning Service. Setting altar calls, attendance, crowd control, offerings, learning and teaching correct ways to catch, were all part of my responsibilities.

So, I was helping this church in Rahway, New Jersey along this line. In that capacity, one Sunday morning when we had a visiting Psalmist Minister in as a special singer and speaker, I was playing head usher. I was standing against the back wall doing my best "Deacon's Stance," standing with my arms folded, with the clicker in my hand and counting heads. While I was doing this and minding my own business, the Lord spoke to me about the visiting minister.

So I went up the side wall of the church and up to the Pastor of the church, who is still a friend of mine to this day. I advised him that I had a WORD for the visiting minister. He acknowledged this fact, and asked me to hold it. He advised me he was about to call a prayer line and that he was going to have the visiting minister join him, and they were going to minister to the whole prayer line together.

He asked me to set the prayer line and work it. Then when they were done ministering to the prayer line he would call me over and hand me the mic, advising the visiting minister that I had a WORD for him. So, I did exactly as the Pastor asked, and when my ushering duties were done, I gave the WORD to the visiting minister. When I was done giving him the WORD, he acknowledged the WORD as being from God, and 100% accurate. He said that everything that I said he was questioning and vacillating about, he had been.

So in this case, even though I had a correct WORD that was publicly acknowledged by the recipient of the WORD, I still had to yield to the Pastor's authority as the 'Set Man' and delegated authority in the house. It was no big deal to hold the WORD until the Pastor was ready for me to release it. Sometimes folks think, *"If I don't do it now, I will lose the WORD."* Nothing could be further from the truth!

RIGHT ALONG THIS LINE WE NEED TO UNDERSTAND delegated authority too. Let's say that the local 'Set Man' in the local church has turned the service over to the worship leader. Now the 'Set Man' is *THE* authority in the local church, but at that moment, he has delegated authority to the worship leader. So at that moment, as long as the worship leader is operating under the delegated authority of the 'Set Man' everyone should be submitted to the worship leader. As long as they are operating in that capacity, if you have something during that time, you should be going to the worship leader because they are the delegated authority at that moment.

Many in this case would still go to the 'Set Man' because he is the supreme authority as the under shepherd in the house. But you see, this is a lack of understanding of delegated authority. Because he has delegated that authority, the 'Set Man' (or woman, there can be ladies that are heads of ministries too), is not in charge until such a time as they take it back. Folks, this is part of protocol.

LET ME TAKE THIS IN ANOTHER DIRECTION WHILE I AM AT it. Several years ago I was a member of a local church called, *Community Church Fixer of Hearts* in North Brunswick, New Jersey. My good friend and Brother, Rev. Barry Habib, was the Pastor of the church. He was the 'Set Man.' I served in the church as a teaching elder and was considered to be a Prophet, and was accepted as a Prophet not just by Pastor Barry, but by the rest of the leadership and the congregation as well.

That being said, I was under Pastor Barry's authority in that house because he was the 'Set Man.' There were times that he had me speak or minister in the house. At those times he delegated authority to me. When I was operating under his delegated authority, folks then looked to me to see if something was right or in order. But once I turned things back over to Pastor Barry, they didn't look to me anymore because I was not operating under delegated authority anymore.

Now let's bring another scenario into this. I also operated *(and still do)* in a parachurch ministry with my parents, Apostles Leo & Edith Fram, called *Living Faith Ministries International* (LFMI for short). Sometimes LFMI held meetings that Pastor Barry would attend. Sometimes we even used the facility of the Community Church Fixer of Hearts building. When Pastor Barry would come to a meeting that we were holding, even if it is in his house, because it was our meeting, he would come in submitted to our authority. There are times that he would get WORDS in our meetings. When that would happen we would delegate authority to him, and he would operate under delegated authority in our meeting *(the same as we operated under his delegated authority in the local church)*.

So in a sense we were equals and peers in the ministry with him functioning as a local Pastor, and I was operating as a Prophet. Yet we learned how to yield to delegated authority, and be in submission to each other's authority depending on whose meeting it is.

Folks, this is a big part of protocol. If we learn these things and practice them, we will see a much greater manifestation of not just the Gifts of the Spirit, but also of Kingdom Alignment.

Flowing In And Receiving From The Prophetic

As we are moving more and more into the Prophetic move of God, we need a better understanding of it. Just as the office of the Apostle is being restored in our day according to Acts 3:21 (the restoration of all things), so is the office of the Prophet.

There is a rhythm and a flow to everything that God does. If we don't learn the flow of God and learn to flow with it no matter what flow it is, we will have a hard time receiving the benefit of it. I remember being in a meeting one night with Dr. Renny McClain where he made this statement: *"There is a rhythm in the Spirit."* I had never heard anyone ever say that before.

When he said that it went off in me like a bomb. He didn't just say it once, but several times, snapping his fingers almost like a cadence: *"There is a rhythm in the*

Spirit." (snapping) *"There is a rhythm in the Spirit."* (snapping)

We must learn to get in line with that rhythm, or that flow. Well, the Prophetic has a flow or rhythm to it, and its flow or rhythm or is different than say an Evangelistic flow or a Pastoral flow. If we don't know how the Prophetic flows, then we will not be able to flow with it, and if we can't flow with it we can't receive the benefits of it!

Scripture has much to say regarding this office, but we will limit ourselves to just three points in this chapter to help us flow in and receive from it. I want us to look at a familiar portion of Scripture, but I want us to look at it from four different translations to help us see and grasp all the nuances of the words. We will use these verses as a foundational text for this chapter:

> *"Do not **quench the Spirit**; do not **despise prophetic utterances**. But **examine everything** carefully; hold fast to that which is good."* **1Thessalonians 5:19-21 NASB** (Emphasis Mine)

> *"Do not **stifle the Holy Spirit**. Do not **scoff at prophecies**, but **test everything** that is said. Hold on to that which is good."* **1Thessalonians 5:19-21 NLT** (Emphasis Mine)

> *"Don't **suppress the Spirit**, and don't **stifle those who have a word from the Master**. On the other hand **don't be gullible**. Check out everything. Keep only what's*

good." **1Thessalonians 5:19-21 MSG** (Emphasis Mine)

"*Do not* **quench (suppress or subdue) the (Holy) Spirit**. *Do not* **spurn the gifts and utterances of the prophets**-*do not* **depreciate prophetic revelations** *nor* **despise inspired instruction or exhortation** *of warning. But* **test and prove** *all things [until you can recognize] what is good; [to that] hold fast."*
1Thessalonians 5:19-21 AMPC (Emphasis Mine)

In Scripture sometimes we are told what to do, and sometimes we are told what not to do. In this text we are being told what not to do. Here we find some DON'TS listed for our instruction. In these three verses we see three things will help us to flow in and receive from the Prophetic move:

1. Don't Quench.
2. Don't Despise.
3. Don't Be Gullible.

I want to look at each one of these three points briefly in this chapter so that we can learn how better to flow with the Prophetic.

Don't Quench

It is important for us to remember that when the Apostle Paul wrote his letters to the churches he had more than one purpose in writing them. Sometimes one of the purposes, was what he was doing in this passage. He was telling them…and us…*what Not To Do*.

If Paul was telling us "Don't" do something, or "Not" to do something, that must mean that we have the ability to do it, or else he would not have said don't do it. The other thing to bear in mind here is, if he says don't do it, and we do…do it, then we will find ourselves out of the rhythm or the flow in that area.

In Verse 19 of this text we see from the different translations we have quoted: 'DON'T QUENCH' 'DON'T STIFLE' 'DON'T SUPPRESS' THE HOLY SPIRIT. For Paul to tell us not to quench the Holy Spirit, that must mean that we have the ability to quench the Holy Spirit. According to Webster's Dictionary, the word QUENCH is defined as: *to stop a fire from burning, to put out a fire, to extinguish.*

Now I don't know about you…but have you ever been in a meeting where it just seemed red hot and ablaze with the move of the Holy Spirit, and then somebody out of ignorance—not knowing what to do or not knowing what not to do—did something that they should not do? And it was like they just threw a bucket of water on the meeting, and that was it. It was done.

I have been in more meetings like that than I wish to have been in. To be honest with you, I don't ever want to be in a meeting like that again. The moment that they did what they should not have done, they did exactly what Paul said not to do. They quenched the Holy Spirit. They threw a bucket of water on the fire. What a letdown that is for us in a meeting, to know that there was more, that God wanted to do more, but the Spirit was quenched, and He could not do what He wanted to do.

My dear Brother and Sister, we must learn how to flow with the Holy Spirit. We must learn how to honor and reverence Him. If we don't, we will quench Him. If we quench Him, we will not see the prophetic move of God.

THE SECOND WORD WE SEE IN THE TRANSLATIONS WE looked at is the word STIFLE. Webster's Dictionary defines stifle as: *to not allow yourself to do or express something; to not allow someone from doing or expressing something.* So when Paul said don't stifle the Holy Spirit, he was saying don't put the Holy Spirit in a strait jacket where He is unable to be God and do what He wants to do. I am constantly amazed by folks in the church who say they want a move of God, and then control everything so tightly that the Holy Spirit couldn't say anything if He wanted to, because He would be out of order.

Now mind you, I totally believe in everything being done decently and in order. But it is possible to have the freedom of the Spirit and maintain order at the same time. Just because you have a move of the Spirit of God does not mean that you are going to have total anarchy and chaos. I don't know why folks think it is one extreme or the other. I remember Brother Hagin used to tell us that folks seem to want to get in the ditch on one side of the road or the other, and the truth is always right down the middle. Boy, I wish we would learn that!

I know I may be dating myself here...but when I hear the word stifle, I can't help but think of Archie Bunker. For those of you old enough to remember the sitcom back in the 70s called: "All In The Family," I am sure you remember what Archie used to say to his wife Edith all the time, *"Edith, stifle yourself!"* What was Archie saying and doing? He was first not honoring his wife. Second he was shutting her down by not allowing her to express herself. We can do exactly the same thing to the Holy Spirit. If we stifle the Holy Spirit, we can forget not just about a move of the Spirit, but in our case, having a Prophetic flow or move in our midst.

THE LAST WORD WE COME ACROSS FROM THE VARIOUS translations that we looked at is the word SUPPRESS. According to Webster's Dictionary, suppress is defined as: *to end or stop something by force, to not allow people to know about or see something.* Do you realize what the Apostle Paul is saying? If we suppress the Holy Spirit, we stop Him by force and/or we don't allow people to see or know about Him.

Sometimes it is not the people's fault that they don't know about the Holy Spirit, it is the Leaderships fault that they don't know about the Holy Spirit, for the Leadership has suppressed Him…stopping Him and/or not allowing the people to know about or see Him in manifestation.

If we don't allow the Holy Spirit to move, how in the world can we ever expect to have the Prophetic flow of God in our churches? Folks let me be as plain as I can be; if you Quench, Stifle and/or Suppress the Holy Spirit, **you are Pathetic not Prophetic!**

I remember when I was a student at Rhema Bible Training Center back in the 80s, Dad Hagin used to tell us: *"The Spirit of God is a Gentleman, He does not go where He is not welcome."* I have to be honest with you folks, I have never been able to improve upon that statement! The Spirit of God is a Gentleman, and He does not go where He is not welcome! Learn it!

Before we move on to our next point I want to share something with you that the Lord brought out by inspiration one day while I was teaching in a "School of the Prophets" seminar. As I was teaching, the Lord quickened to me 1Corinthians chapter 11, which I am sure many of you know to be the passage that the

Apostle Paul gives his instruction on the Lord's Table or Communion.

> *"But let a man examine himself, and so let him eat of the bread and drink of the cup. For he who eats and drinks in an unworthy manner eats and drinks judgment to himself,* **not discerning the Lord's body***. For this reason many are weak and sick among you, and many sleep."* **1Corinthians 11: 28-30** (Emphasis Mine)

> *"But a man must examine himself, and in so doing he is to eat of the bread and drink of the cup. For he who eats and drinks, eats, and drinks judgment to himself* **if he does not judge the body rightly***. For this reason many among you are weak and sick, and a number sleep."* **1Corinthians 11: 28-30 NASB** (Emphasis Mine)

This is a familiar portion of Scripture that many churches use when preparing to observe the Lord's Table. I want you to pay attention to the phrases highlighted in the two translations quoted: *"not discerning the Lord's body"* and *"if he does not judge the body rightly"*. I would like to make a composite of the two of those and say, **not discerning the Lord's body rightly.**

WHO IS THE BODY OF CHRIST? THE EPISTLES ARE CLEAR that we are the body of Christ and members in particular (see 1Corinthians 12:27). It also says that God has placed or set us in the body as He pleased or as He desired (see

1Corinthians 12:18). It also says that we being many are one body in Christ and individually members of one another (see Romans 12:5).

So we could look at judging the Lord's Body as judging one another, since we are the Body of Christ. This takes on a whole new meaning. Now let me give you a practical example of how this works in everyday life. In the local church where I am part of the Leadership team, one of the ladies, the Pastor's wife, besides being a teacher is also both a Seer (Seeing Prophet, having dreams and visions) and a Prophetess (speaking by inspiration and revelation).

Now let's say for argument's sake that I look at her and I say: Well she is a teacher, but I don't think she is a Seer/Prophetess! Now if God has set her, if God has placed her as a Seer/Prophetess in the body, but I don't receive her as God has placed her, as God has set her, as God has gifted her, do you see how I could be guilty of not discerning the Lord's Body rightly?

Folks that is a dangerous place to be, when you don't receive people as God has placed them, as God has gifted them. In essence you are saying, *"Holy Spirit, You made a mistake by putting them in that position."* Like the robot in the 1960s science fiction TV show "Lost In Space" used to say: *"Danger! Danger!"* I don't want to find myself arguing or fighting against God.

Can you see how this type of action would quench the Spirit, stifle the Spirit, or suppress the Spirit? We must avoid this at all costs if we want to flow in the Prophetic. Not only must we honor the Holy Spirit, but we must honor one another as God has gifted and set each one so that we may be the recipient of their gifting. A great principle we need to learn that I learned from Dr. Mike Brown is: *"What you honor you draw to you, what you dishonor you push away from you."*

Don't Despise

From the different translations of verse 20, we have quoted we see:

- Don't Despise Prophetic Utterances
- Don't Scoff At Prophecies
- Don't Stifle Those Who Have A Word From The Master
- Don't Spurn The Gifts And Utterances Of The Prophets
- Don't Depreciate Prophetic Revelations
- Don't Despise Inspired Instruction Or Exhortation.

Again it is important for us to remember that if the Apostle Paul is telling us not to do something, that must mean that we have the ability to do that thing, or else he would not tell us not to do it. Another thing to bear in mind is that many times in his writings to the churches, Paul was writing to correct some error or errors that were prevalent within the church that he was writing to. In that respect his correction to the church at Thessalonica would be applicable to us today.

Could you imagine that the Apostle Paul would have to write to the church to **not** DESPISE Prophetic Utterance? To me that seems just unthinkable, especially in light of what the word DESPISE means. Webster's Dictionary defines despise like this: *to dislike (something or someone) very much; to look down on with contempt or aversion; to regard as negligible, worthless, or distasteful.* Now after looking at all of those meanings for the word DESPISE, it is clear that Paul was saying something pretty strong.

How could anybody in the church dislike Prophecy very much? How could we look down on it with contempt or think it was negligible? How could we think that Prophecy was worthless or distasteful? Yet this is the attitude that Paul was writing to correct.

But we can go on. The New Living Translation used the word SCOFF. Webster's Dictionary defines scoff as: *an expression of scorn, derision, or contempt; an object of scorn, mockery, or derision.* That MOCKERY is the one that gets me. Mockery means to make fun of. I can't imagine anyone making fun of the Prophetic, can you? But yet Paul is admonishing us not to do it.

Then we come to The Message Translation, which said don't STIFLE those who have a word from the master. We have already looked at the word stifle in the previous section; which meant to not allow yourself to do or express something; to not allow someone from doing or expressing something. Can you imagine not allowing someone who has a word from the Master to give the word that they have? Selah!

Then we come to The Amplified Classic, which hits us with the words: spurn, depreciate and again the word despise. SPURN is not a word we use every day now is it? Webster's Dictionary defines spurn as: *to refuse to accept (someone or something that you do not think deserves your respect, attention, affection, etc.); to tread sharply or heavily upon; to reject with disdain or contempt.* So we are not to spurn or refuse to accept, or reject with disdain the gifts and utterances of the Prophets. Yikes!

Then we come to, don't depreciate prophetic revelations. Webster defines DEPRECIATE as: *to decrease in value; to describe (something) as having little value; to lower in estimation or esteem.* So when Paul said not to depreciate prophetic revelations; he was saying not to decrease the value of them, or to not lower your esteem for them, or to not see them as having little or no value. Are you getting the seriousness of what the Apostle Paul is saying about our attitudes toward the Prophetic?

The last thing The Amplified Classic touched on was the word DESPISE again. Paul said don't despise inspired instruction or exhortation. I want you to notice that Paul is talking about those words that are **INSPIRED**, which means they are from God. We are not talking about something that came from too much pepperoni pizza here. Again, DESPISE carries that meaning of disliking something very much, I would dare say it even borders on hate. How could anyone despise the real genuine Prophetic?

I WANT TO ADDRESS SOME THINGS HERE THAT MAYBE ARE not quite as pronounced as these things are the way the Apostle Paul brings them out in Scripture. Yet they are quite akin and closely related, just a little more subtle. Maybe you might say to me, *"Well Mike, I really don't hate the Prophetic, I just don't think much of it."* Have you ever heard in all of your years in the Kingdom: *"Oh that's no big deal, that's just a Prophecy?"* Or have you heard, *"Well, old Brother so and so is just Prophesying again?"*

Well I sure have! And every time I do I have this sudden urge to be like Leroy Jethro Gibbs in the TV show *NCIS* and give somebody what he normally gives (a smack upside the head) to Tony DiNozzo. Does anybody know what I am talking about? I just feel that Gibbs anointing is coming on me when I hear statements like that! **How dare we say, "That's just a Prophecy?"**

Folks, if you think it is no big deal, that it is just a Prophecy…then you need to get a revelation of what Prophecy really is! What do we mean when we say, *"Well, old Brother so and so is just Prophesying again?"* Thank God, old Brother so and so is doing it, and if you had half a brain you would want to do it too. Didn't the word say: *"Pursue love, yet desire earnestly spiritual gifts,* **but especially that you may prophesy**"? **1Corinthians 14:1 NASB** (Emphasis Mine) We are supposed to want to Prophesy!

I want to delve into another area that I have touched upon briefly, but I want to hit it a little harder. This is one area that really bothers me with many circles in the Body of Christ. Even those that somewhat believe in the Prophetic are guilty of this one. Have you ever heard anywhere in any circle: "Well you are not part of the leadership, so you can't Prophesy here"? How about pulling a Scripture that says know those that labor among you so far out of context that you give the Word of God a hermeneutical hernia?

> How did The Message put it? "*...and don't **stifle those who have a word from the Master...**"
> Is that plain enough for you?
> But you are not part of this house. "*...and don't **stifle those who have a word from the Master...**"
> But you have not been recognized. "*...and don't **stifle those who have a word from the Master...**"

Are you hearing me? If we have practices that are contrary to Scripture, we can forget about having the Prophetic Move of God in our house.

Now I am not saying that we don't follow protocol. I am not saying we don't have things done decently and in order. We have already dealt with those issues in this book quite clearly. We are to be submitted to

God and to God-ordained authority. However, I am tired of controlling leaders who don't or won't empower and allow the people of God to exercise and operate in the things that God has anointed and gifted them for.

Too many are just afraid that someone is going to make a mistake, and then they are going to have to fix and correct the mistake. So rather than be a spiritual father that is empowering, training, and raising up the next generation; we sit like a superstar Christian that others should want to be like, all the while keeping them in bondage and ourselves contrary to New Testament practice. You might say, *"Mike you are being awfully strong; how can you make such dogmatic statements?"*

Because I can read what the New Testament pattern for church life should resemble:

> *"What is the outcome then, brethren? When you assemble,* **each one** *has a psalm, has a teaching, has a revelation, has a tongue, has an interpretation. Let all things be done for edification."*
> **1Corinthians 14:26 NASB** (Emphasis Mine)

Each one is the key phrase in that verse. Each one should have something to contribute.

> *"For* **you can all prophesy** *one by one, so that all may learn, and all may be exhorted."* **1Corinthians 14:31 NASB** (Emphasis Mine)

How many can Prophesy? You can all Prophesy!

But you are not part of the leadership. *"...and don't **stifle those who have a word from the Master...**"*

Folks let's be honest, some of us have some practices we need to correct. We have not been paying attention to the Apostle Paul's "DON'TS".

I have found that the greatest flow and stream of the Prophetic with the greatest revelation comes in an atmosphere where not only is it welcomed, but people are encouraged to participate. That is an atmosphere of love, unity, and instruction that the Spirit of God delights to manifest Himself in.

If we have indifference towards the gifts of the Spirit in general, and specifically towards prophetic utterance, we can forget about having a move of God in the church. There will not be a Prophetic stream in our midst. You can't stop the flow and the stream by your attitudes and your actions, and then think that your prayers for it will override those attitudes and actions that you have already displayed. Those attitudes and actions will nullify your prayer. Turn it around and open your services to whomever God desires to use and just see what God will do.

Don't Be Gullible

From Verse 21 in the different translations we quoted we see:

- Examine Everything Carefully
- Test Everything That Is Said
- Don't Be Gullible, Check Out Everything
- Test And Prove All Things.

It is important for us to understand that we are capable of being gullible, believing every prophetic word as being from God, or else Paul would not have warned us not to be. Just as we are not to be indifferent toward or despising of Prophetic Words, we must also not be foolish. Just because someone says 'thus saith the Lord', does it mean that it is from God?

How many times have you heard supposed Prophetic Words that you said to yourself, *"There is no way that is from God"*? We have clear-cut Scriptural guidelines for prophetic words. Here, we are told to examine them, test them, check them out and prove them. John said:

> *"Dear friends,* **do not believe everyone who claims to speak by the Spirit.** *You must* **test them to see if the spirit they have comes from God.** *For* **there are many false prophets in the world.** *This is the way to find out if they have the Spirit of God: If a prophet acknowledges that Jesus Christ became a human being, that person has the Spirit of God. If a prophet does not acknowledge*

Jesus, that person is not from God..." **1John 4:1-3a NLT**
(Emphasis Mine)

I am not sure how we came to the idea that we are not to judge WORDS. John clearly states that we are to 'Test' them to see if it is from God. To me that does not sound like we are not supposed to judge, it sounds like we are! Paul said:

> *"But one who* ***prophesies speaks to men for edification and exhortation and consolation."***
> **1Corinthians 14:3 NASB**

Again, we see the edification, exhortation, and comfort, or consolation test. Just because someone says: *"My Little Children", "So Says The Lord", The Lord Would Say Unto Thee,"* or some other accepted "Prophetic Verbiage", **that does not mean that the Lord said!** We can't be Gullible!

Prophecies will always line up with the Word of God. They will never contradict it. Personal prophecies will usually confirm what is already in your spirit; it will rarely be new revelation to you. There should always be a witness in your spirit of the 'Word' received.

Obviously there is a genuine prophetic gifting and move of God. We must be careful to not quench the Spirit of God and shut Him down so He cannot flow through this vital ministry to the church. At the same time we can never take lightly when He does minister to us through prophetic ministry. In fact, we must seek for it, not despise it. Yet we must remain balanced in our pursuit of the prophetic, and not be so foolish as to believe that every supposed prophetic word is from God. **We must test them to make sure that they are. As we do, we will flow with this move.**

Levels Of Prophetic Gifting

Back somewhere around the year 2000 or 2001, I was in my own transition from functioning as an Evangelist to functioning as a Prophet. During that time one of the books that really helped was titled, *How To Develop Your Prophetic Gifting*, by Graham Cooke.[1]

In this book the author makes a statement to the effect that every Spirit-filled Christian can prophesy, but that does not make everyone who does a Prophet. He goes on to talk about the many levels or stages of development in PROPHETIC GIFTING that one goes through from just operating in the manifestation gift of prophecy all the way to functioning in the ministry gift of Prophet *I am paraphrasing from my memory here; this is not an exact quote).*

One of the other things that stood out to me about this quote from Brother Cooke was the timeframe involved to move or go through all the levels or stages of prophetic gifting, from prophecy to Prophet. He had found that the mentoring, training, and discipling that one had received had a direct bearing on how quickly one moved through the levels or stages, but the average was 15-20 years.

In teaching along these lines since the late 2000's, I have always followed this thought from Graham Cooke with my own statement that goes right along with it: *"Every Prophet will prophesy, but not everyone who does is a Prophet."*

There are four general levels of PROPHETIC GIFTING that we will discuss in this chapter.

- The Simple Gift of Prophecy
- Some Prophetic Gifting
- The Prophetic Ministry
- The Office of a Prophet

Rev. Kenneth E. "Dad" Hagin always used the term: *"the simple gift of prophecy"* in his teachings *(which I was privileged to hear in person many times through my two years at Rhema, as well as in his books and syllabi)*, to describe the first level of PROPHETIC GIFTING. Graham Cooke in his book referred to that same level as *"the shallow end of basic prophecy"*.

This level is the starting place where every believer starts. Nobody starts out functioning as an ascension gift Prophet (Ministry Gift of Prophet), even though they may be ultimately called to be one. *(See Ephesians chapter 4, Prophet was one of the gifts Jesus gave to the Church when He ascended up on high.)* Thinking this would be like thinking one could start with Algebra in mathematics without first learning $2 + 2 = 4$.

This beginning level of gifting, The Simple Gift of Prophecy, would be the manifestation gift of Prophecy that we find in 1Corinthians chapter 12. There are a total of nine Manifestations of the Spirit listed in that context, which many call the Gifts of the Holy Spirit. This manifestation of the Spirit is what we dealt with in great detail in chapter two of this book.

Moving on from The Simple Gift Of Prophecy, one comes to the second level of prophetic gifting, Some Prophetic Gifting. Some might also call a person at this level of development, a Prophetic Person. Either term would work here, it is just a matter of personal preference. A person who is at this level of prophetic gifting would be someone that exercises the Gift of Prophecy more than just occasionally.

Another characteristic of someone at this level of prophetic development would be someone that receives prophetic revelation from Words of Knowledge or Words of Wisdom through either dreams, visions, an inner witness of the Spirit in their spirit, or the still small voice of the Holy Spirit; maybe even [what might seem to be] an audible voice of God [however God normally communicates with that person], as most folks have a predominate way that God communicates with them.

A person at this level would not necessarily be a Minister. They might even be considered (as much as I hate this term) a *layperson*, meaning they are not in the ministry.

This person would also have greater revelation and authority than someone that just exercises the SIMPLE GIFT OF PROPHECY occasionally.

MOVING ON FROM SOME PROPHETIC GIFTING, ONE would move to the next level we call, THE PROPHETIC MINISTRY. This particular level of prophetic gifting manifests in a few ways. Let me lay out some of the most likely scenarios. First might be someone that we would consider one of the other three ascension gift ministers besides Apostle or Prophet: Evangelist, Pastor, or Teacher. They would believe in both Apostles and Prophets, and operate consistently in the manifestation gifts of the Holy Spirit.

A second scenario might be a Minister that operates in either the Revelation Gifts of the Spirit (Word of Knowledge, Word of Wisdom, Discerning of Spirits) and/or the Inspiration Gifts of the Spirit (Prophecy, Tongues, The Interpretation of Tongues) regularly.

A third scenario might be a person that has the ultimate call to be a Five-Fold Ascension Gift Prophet, but is still in a process of development toward being ready to be commissioned to stand in the fullness of the office.

A fourth scenario might be a person who has been recognized and noted for operating in their Prophetic gifting by seasoned, mature leaders.

Even as a person at level two, SOME PROPHETIC GIFTING had greater revelation and authority in the Spirit than someone at level one, THE SIMPLE GIFT OF PROPHECY, so this person at level three, THE PROPHETIC MINISTRY (or a Prophetic Minister) will have greater revelation and authority in the Spirit than either of the first two levels of prophetic gifting.

The final level of PROPHETIC GIFTING is the OFFICE OF THE PROPHET. Of course, this is also known as the Five-Fold Ministry Gift of a Prophet, or the ascension gift of a Prophet. This is the subject of the next chapter in this book so kindly turn the page for an in-depth look at the Prophet.

---

1. *Published by Sovereign World Limited October 1, 2000*

The Office Of The Prophet

As we begin to consider the office of the Prophet, I believe it is imperative that we refer back to the statement previously paraphrased (not quoted exactly) from Graham Cooke about the time period involved and the various stages one goes through from what he called, the shallow end of basic prophecy (what Rev. Kenneth E. "Dad" Hagin) referred to as (the simple gift of Prophecy) all the way up to the office of a Prophet. How many years on average that it takes, depending on the mentoring, training, and discipling one has received.

I also want to remind you of my quote: *"All Prophets Will Prophesy, But Not All Who Prophesy Are Prophets!"*

Having stated both of those points again, now we can begin to lay our doctrinal foundation from the Epistles, or Paul the Apostle.

> *"And He gave some as **Apostles**, and some as **Prophets**, and some as **Evangelists**, and some as **Pastors** and **Teachers**."* **Ephesians 4:11 NASB** (Emphasis Mine)
>
> *"Having been built upon the **foundation** of the **Apostles** and **Prophets**, Christ Jesus Himself being the cornerstone."* **Ephesians 2:20 NASB** (Emphasis Mine)
>
> *"And God has appointed in the church, first **Apostles**, second **Prophets**, third **Teachers**, then miracles, then Gifts of Healings, helps, administrations, various kinds of tongues."* **1Corinthians 12:28 NASB** *(*Emphasis Mine*)*

A Prophet is one of the five-fold ministry offices or gifts. (some also refer to these gifts as the Ascension Gifts of Christ or of Jesus, a term I personally prefer to use). But you can use Five-Fold Ministry, Ministry Gifts, or Ascension Gifts to refer to these five ministry graces, I am fine with whichever term you prefer.

In 1Corinthians 12:28 we see that Apostles are appointed or set (depending on the translation) as first, while Prophets are second. The word for FIRST in the original Greek that the New Testament was written in, carries the meaning of first in rank, order, or succession. This is not in a hierarchal sense, as in the top of the totem pole, or the most important. But Apostle was the first gift that Jesus set when He began His church. Remember He called twelve that they might be with Him, and then He named them as Apostles.

When we look at the word second, in 1Corinthians 12:28 in the Original Greek, it carries the meaning of being –

'the other of two.' This means that it is just like the first. I like to look at Apostles and Prophets, to use some modern vernacular, as 'kissing cousins'. Or if you watched Saturday morning cartoons when I was growing up, 'Wonder Twins', or 'Power Twins.'

Because we have so conflated the issue of Prophets and Prophecy, still way too many in the church believe that they are one and the same, and nothing could be further from the truth! So, let me just state plainly that prophecy is only part of what a Prophet does.

I was privileged in my life to sit at the feet of Rev. Kenneth E. "Dad" Hagin for two years at Rhema. He recounted for us several times about one of the encounters where the Lord Jesus appeared to him, pulling up a chair, and teaching him about the office of the Prophet. Dad Hagin did also write about this encounter in many of his books, so if you have read a lot of his books you might remember what I am about to tell you.

According to the Lord to Dad Hagin, a Prophet first of all will be either a preacher or a teacher, or both first! As a five-fold ascension gift, a Prophet has the responsibility of Equipping, Edifying, Unifying, Maturing, and Stabilizing the Body of Christ along with the other ascension gifts according to the context of Ephesians, Chapter 4.

How can one do that without teaching and or preaching? Also, if according to Ephesians 2:20, that the church is built on the foundation of Apostles and Prophets, what kind of foundation would the church have if one-half of it could not teach or preach?

THIS IDEA THAT IS RUNNING RAMPANT IN THE CHURCH today, that all a Prophet does is go around giving Prophetic Words, is absolutely absurd! When one of my spiritual daughters, that I did commission as a Prophet, was nearing the end of her process and getting close to her time of commissioning, I advised her that there was still one thing that she was lacking. I told her she needed to develop her teaching and preaching gifts, because she could not be a Prophet without that being in place first.

Thank God she did not take offense to this instruction as so many easily do in our day. Rather she asked what to do. I advised her to purchase and read two books: *Prescription For Preaching*[1] and *How To Prepare Sermons*.[2] I also gave her my whole sermon outline folder to study. I told her I didn't care if she preached my messages, but I wanted her to study the format of them so that she could duplicate the format. Finally, I advised her that she needed to start teaching and preaching on her Internet broadcasts as opposed to just interviewing guests that she had on.

I am so grateful that she listened to all of my instructions and applied herself to all of them. She began to develop her teaching and preaching. So much so, that I have a spiritual son that sometimes watches her broadcasts, and he said to me, *"Dad, I was watching my Sister (since they are both my spiritual children, she would be his sister), and she began to preach, and she sounded like you!"* **Because she had developed in this area,** I knew she was ready to be commissioned as a Prophet...**and not before.**

THE NEXT THING THAT THE LORD TOLD DAD HAGIN about the Prophet's office was: *"A Prophet will have the Gift of Prophecy fully developed in their life, and it will operate consistently in their ministry."* I add to this: At a much higher level of Prophetic Gifting than SIMPLE GIFT OF PROPHECY, SOME PROPHETIC GIFTING, or PROPHETIC MINISTRY.

I wish to draw attention to the fact that the Lord told Dad Hagin that a Prophet would have the Gift of Prophecy, 'Fully Developed'! This means you can't be a newcomer, or novice in exercising the Gift of Prophecy. This gift must be fully developed in one's life if they are to stand in the office of the Prophet.

Secondly, I wish to draw attention to the fact that the Lord said that the Gift of Prophecy would operate **consistently** (not sporadically or occasionally). Today, just because somebody prophesies once or twice, folks want to go and make them a Prophet. **No.** The gift MUST operate consistently in the life of the one that is the stand in the Prophet's office.

The next thing the Lord told Dad Hagin about the Prophet's office was that: *"A Prophet will receive revelation* *from two or more of the Revelation Gifts of the Holy Spirit consistently in their ministry."* Of course the three Revelation Gifts of the Holy Spirit are: The Word Of Knowledge, The Word Of Wisdom, and The Discerning of Spirits.

PLEASE ALLOW ME TO CONTINUE WITH SOME OF MY OWN bullet points if you will, as well as some others I have amassed through the years from other sources (not sure where some of them came from) concerning the Function of the Prophet.

- A Prophet will receive greater revelation than any of the other three levels of prophetic gifting that we have already looked at and will speak with much greater authority in the Spirit.
- A Prophet will accurately proclaim through preaching, teaching, and/or prophesying what God is saying at that moment to specific local assemblies, regions, or individuals.
- Because of this function, the Prophet literally becomes the mouthpiece of God.
- It should also be noted that a Prophet should have a proven track record for being accurate and right.

I can hear someone ask if there is Biblical proof of that? Thanks for asking.

Does anyone remember a Prophet named Agabus in the book of Acts? In Acts chapter 11, he predicted a great famine that came to pass. Then we see Agabus in Acts 21, where he takes Paul's belt and binds his own hands and feet with it. Then he announces that the Holy Spirit was saying that the Jews in Jerusalem would do the same to the owner of that belt. Because of Agabus' track record for being correct about the famine, they took it as fact concerning Paul going to Jerusalem.

So much so that the people began to entreat Paul that he should not go. I have heard many folks say that this was a warning that Paul should not go. I beg to differ. The Word of the Lord was not that Paul should not go, but that this would befall him when he got there. Doesn't the Bible teach that the Holy Spirit would show us things to come? So this was not, "DON'T GO!" This is about this is going to happen when you do go.

Personally I believe Agabus was operating by the Word of Wisdom, releasing it through Prophecy, to show Paul what was to come. This brings me to my next point. A Prophet, because he speaks by both inspiration and revelation, will both foretell and forth tell, where the SIMPLE GIFT OF PROPHECY is just forth-telling, because there is no revelation contained within it.

WHEN WE LOOKED AT THE SIMPLE GIFT OF PROPHECY, IT was merely speaking by inspiration, according to 1Corinthians 14:3, Edification, Exhortation, and/or

Comfort, whereas Prophets speak by both Inspiration as well as Revelation from the Revelation Gifts of the Spirit. Just so we are all on the same page, allow me to give basic definitions of the three Revelation Gifts.

> **Word of Knowledge** – The Gift of The Word of Knowledge is a supernatural revelation by the Holy Spirit of a fact or facts in the mind of God in either the past or present.
> **Word of Wisdom** - The Gift of The Word of Wisdom is a supernatural revelation by the Holy Spirit concerning the divine purpose and plan in the mind and will of God about the future.
> **Discerning of Spirits** - The Discerning of Spirits is a supernatural revelation by the Holy Spirit into the spirit realm. It can bring insight into three different types of spirits: Divine…God or angels, Demonic…the devil or demons, Human…that is to reveal the motives or tendencies of someone's heart or spirit.

So what we find with a Prophet when they prophesy, many times in contrast to just the gift of Prophecy, is that the Prophet will release either The Word of Knowledge, or The Word of Wisdom through the vehicle of the Gift or Prophecy. Remember the Word of Knowledge deals with the present and/or the past, where the Word of Wisdom deals with that which is yet unborn, about the purpose and destiny of God in the future.

In essence they are still speaking by Inspiration, because one cannot Prophesy without the Inspiration of the Holy Spirit, but are now incorporating Revelation into their Prophetic Word. And in the most simplistic form, it will be something along the lines of: *"This is where you are... this is where you've been...and this is where God wants you to go!"*

Next, a Prophet will have the matured wisdom of God that has come through experience and relationship with the Holy Spirit. Again, this shows us the picture of a seasoned leader, not a novice. There must be a wealth of experience from years of walking with Holy Spirit if one is to be considered a Prophet.

Here is one that might actually cause us to question many of the self-proclaimed and self-appointed 'Prophets' we see all over social media these days. A Prophet will have godly character, having developed the fruit of the spirit in his or her life.

Have you ever read this verse in 1Corinthians, Chapter 14?

> *"And the spirits of the prophets are subject to the prophets."*
> **1Corinthians 14:32 NKJV**

I don't know how many times I have heard folks say that they just could not help themselves, that the Spirit moved them, so they did something out of order, like prophesy while the Preacher was preaching, or prophesy while somebody else was Prophesying.

So the Preacher is the delegated authority, and so Holy Spirit is going to prompt you to Prophesy and interrupt the delegated authority? Right! **I don't think so.**

So someone is Prophesying, but your word is more important than theirs, so Holy Spirit prompts you to speak while they are speaking? Right! **I don't think so.**

That does not sound like

> *"For you can all prophesy one by one..."* **1 Corinthians 14:31a NASB**

WHAT WE HAVE TODAY IS MANY THAT LACK SELF-control, which is part of the fruit of the Spirit. Then because they haven't developed the fruit of the Spirit in their lives, they can't even follow the instructions from Paul that everything must be done decently and in order (1 Corinthians 14:40). No, your spirit is subject to you. You blurted out, out of order because you wanted to. Don't blame the Holy Ghost because you don't have self-control!

Here is another thought that many don't consider, but which is crucial to the ministry and assignment of a Prophet. A primary concern for the Prophet is to get not just the vision of God, but also the heartbeat of God and communicate it to His people. I believe sometimes we forget that God too has feelings and emotions that run not just as deep as ours do, but more deeply than ours do. Prophets must not only see as God sees, but also feel as God feels, communicating both to His people.

Now I want to deal with somewhat of a deeper prophetic issue that many in today's prophetic movement don't really believe in. I want to talk about both DIRECTIVE and CORRECTIVE prophetic words. In speaking about the Gift of Prophecy earlier in this book, we did mention these two types of 'Words'. Why do I say that many don't really believe in them? Because they overemphasize 1Corinthians 14:3. This of course is the verse that speaks of Prophecy speaking unto men for Edification, Exhortation, and Comfort.

As many cannot see a DIRECTIVE or CORRECTIVE PROPHECY in the framework of that verse, they won't or don't receive this type of PROPHETIC WORD. I often say that Prophets are not bound by those criteria of 1Corinthians 14:3, **Prophecy is.** BIG DIFFERENCE!

In fact, it is the Prophet that this type of WORD will come through most of the time! I am not saying that a DIRECTIVE or CORRECTIVE WORD can't or won't come through a Prophetic Minister (level 3 of prophetic gifting) or another Ascension Gift. But most of the time, it will come through the Prophet. **This function is part of the Prophet's Mantle.**

Prophets are forerunners of change. They prepare the way for a fresh awakening of God. They prophesy life where there is none. They prepare hearts for special visitations from on high. Prophets speak with tremendous authority. The messages that come from their mouths are charged with the anointing and creative power of God for two reasons:

1. The destruction of the kingdom of Satan, and
2. The establishment of the kingdom of God.

I am reminded of the Prophetic Commission to Jeremiah:

> *"'Before I shaped you in the womb, I knew all about you. Before you saw the light of day, I had holy plans for you: A prophet to the nations— that's what I had in mind for you.' God reached out, touched my mouth, and said, 'Look! I've just put my words in your mouth—hand-delivered! See what I've done? I've given you a job to do among nations and governments—a red-letter day! Your job is to pull up and tear down, take apart and demolish, And then start over, building and planting.'"* **Jeremiah 1:5, 9 & 10 The Message**

Prophets are gifted by God to see, hear, or sense (maybe a combination or all of these) what goes on in the spirit realm. Through their spiritual discernment they can tell what the climate or the atmosphere of a service, meeting, room, area, or even a region may be.

Prophets have a tendency to attack the status quo, because they see and know God's purpose and realize that His people are settling for much less than God intends for them. Nothing will irritate a Prophet more than Status Quo Christianity.

In fact, in 2001, when I was functioning as a Prophet, I wrote an article for our Quarterly Newsletter called: "Status Quo Christianity". In that article I said that I had a **Holy Distain for Status Quo Christianity**! That sounds just like a Prophet.

PROPHETS MUST BE CAREFUL TO AVOID PROPHETIC frustration, which will cause the Prophet to become irritated at the people, and his words will harass instead of encouraging the people. PROPHETIC FRUSTRATION is a real thing that Prophets have to deal with day in and day out. When folks are not applying themselves, or pressing in for more, or being satisfied with much less, or settling for where they are, the Prophet gets frustrated. **But they can never take that frustration out on the people.**

This is where longsuffering comes in. This is where the Prophet must remind themselves that grace and mercy must be extended to the people, even as The Master has many times extended grace and mercy to them. Let's close this chapter with a couple of illustrations showing the prophet in relation to the other Ascension Gifts.

The most well-known illustration is that of the hand. The thumb represents the Apostle because the thumb can easily touch all the other fingers on the hand easily. The pointer finger represents the Prophet because the pointer finger points the way. The middle finger, because it extends out further than any other finger on the hand represents the Evangelist because the Evangelist reaches out more than any other gift. The ring finger is the lover, the place where the wedding band goes. It therefore represents the Pastor, because the Pastor is the lover of the sheep. The pinky being the smallest finger, represents the Teacher, because it is the only one that is small enough to fit in your ear, which is what the Teacher does.

Another illustration of the Five-Fold Ministry is comparing it to a railroad:

The Apostle is the tracklayer, charting the course for the ministry. The Prophet is the engineer, keeping the train on the right track, and the fireman keeping the engine stoked. The Evangelist is the conductor who keeps getting off the train, inviting everybody "All Aboard". The Pastor is the porter who cares for the needs and comfort of the passengers. The Teacher is the tour guide who explains the sights and sounds along the way.

***

Another illustration can be taken from the army:

The General = The Apostle
The Advisors = The Prophets,
Spies = Mature Intercessors
Boot Camp Sergeants = Teachers
Recruiters = Evangelists
Medic/Chaplains = Pastors

The General (Apostle) develops a Strategy/Battle Plan for War. He meets with his Advisors (Prophets) to further develop his plan. He will then adjust it according to their input: for example, Timing and Direction. The Advisors bring their knowledge of the War. Then they add to that the information that the Spies (Mature Intercessors) bring them.

The Spies go out and gather information to bring to the General's Advisors (Prophets). The Boot Camp Sergeants (Teachers) fit their Training to the Strategy. In this way they will properly equip and train the Troops for battle. The Medic/Chaplains (Pastors) take care of the Troops.

The Recruiters (Evangelists) are out on the street and using media, etcetera to bring in new recruits.

---

1. Fosdick, Harry Emerson. *Prescription for Preaching*. Grand Rapids: Baker Book House, 1980.
2. Evans, William. *How to Prepare Sermons*. Moody Publishers. June 1, 1964.

Special Areas Of The Prophetic

In this chapter we will consider some special areas that would be considered part of the Prophetic Movement or of Prophetic Ministry, but not necessarily one of the four levels of Prophetic Gifting that we have already considered. Bishop Bill Hamon in his writings has drawn attention to things like: 'THE SPIRIT OF PROPHECY, A PROPHETIC PRESBYTERY, PROPHETIC INTERCESSION, 'PROPHETIC SONG, and PROPHETIC EVANGELISM among others. We will devote a little attention to each one of these special areas of the prophetic in this chapter.

THE SPIRIT OF PROPHECY – OUR SCRIPTURAL BASIS FOR this is found in the book of Revelation.

"...For the testimony of Jesus is the spirit of prophecy."
Revelation 19:10c NASB

This is not so much a gift or office, but rather an anointing of the Holy Spirit that allows people who do not normally prophesy, to prophesy. (Really any believer in the room could prophesy whether they have the gift of prophecy or not if they would just press into it.) This often happens under one of three conditions:

1. A mighty prophetic presence of the Lord permeates the service, making it easier to prophesy than to keep silent. (Most common)
2. People come among a company of prophets (King Saul in the OT), or under the mantle of an anointed prophet.
3. People are challenged by a minister to let God arise and testify through them by the spirit of prophecy.

Those that prophesy under these conditions should not assume that they have the Gift of Prophecy or are called to the office of the Prophet, however if they get accustomed to pressing in and exercising in the Gift of Prophecy as the spirit of prophecy is evident, they may develop into one of the four general levels of prophetic gifting.

A Prophetic Presbytery — Our scriptural basis for this comes from 1 Timothy, chapter four.

> *"Do not neglect the spiritual gift within you, which was bestowed upon you through prophetic utterance with the laying on of hands by the presbytery."* **1 Timothy 4:14 NASB**

In defining a Prophetic Presbytery it should be noted that it is not a ritual, nor is it a rite of passage; it is however, a time of impartation, separation, and dedication to the area of service that God has called the individual to. It would be when a group of ministers with advanced levels of prophetic gifting would be laying their hands on and prophesying to an individual or individuals for the purpose of:

1. Prophetic revelation and confirmation of those called to leadership ministry in the church.
2. Ordination to the five-fold ministry. This is for public recognition and authorization as an ordained minister of God.
3. Confirmation and activation of membership ministries in the body of Christ.

All ministers and others in church leadership can exercise their faith and speak a word of prophecy over an individual while functioning as a presbytery team member.

PROPHETIC INTERCESSION / PROPHETIC PRAYER – My dear Sister, Apostle Angie Dorman in teaching many years ago about Prophetic Intercession described it as: *"When the Prophetic and Priestly Ministries Intersect."* I kind of like that definition!

In reality it is when one uses specific Prophetic Revelation in prayer. This revelation can come through a variety of ways including dreams, visions, trances, having it bubble up in your spirit (the essence of the Hebrew word for Prophet – "NABI", which means to bubble up), or hearing the voice of the Lord or Holy Spirit either internally or audibly; or any combination of these, for many times, certain prophetic folks receive their revelations more than one way.

Here are some types of examples of how Prophetic Intercession could be utilized:

1. Knowing what the controlling spirit is over a territory so you can take authority over it.
2. Knowing the purpose and plan of God for a person, ministry, city, state, or nation and calling forth that purpose and plan in prayer.
3. Knowing ahead of time of a plot of the enemy against a person, ministry, city, state, or nation and canceling the assignment before it arrives.

I would also like to consider PROPHETIC PRAYER in this chapter which is closely related to PROPHETIC INTERCESSION. Prophetic Prayer could be described as not coming with a list of things to be prayed, that you check off as you go through the list, but rather that **you come to get the list to pray.** It could also be considered as praying the Father's heart back to Him.

At its very core, prayer is a dialogue, not a monologue. It is not just us talking to Him, but also allowing Him to talk back to us. In times past, many of us would make our plans and then ask God to bless them. In prophetic prayer we find out what His plans are and then they are already blessed.

AS WE HAVE SO MANY THAT ARE DEVELOPING IN prophetic gifting either from Seer (visual) gifting by either visions, dreams, or trances; or from Nabi (bubbles up) gifting by either an inward witness, inward voice, or inner promptings; they can take that revelation and instead of speaking out, they can pray it out.

When we pray prophetically, we lay down our own imaginations, desires, and burdens; and depend on Him to show us what is on His agenda. He reveals to us what He would have us to pray. Most of the time prophetic prayer is born out of praying in the Spirit (your prayer language, or praying in tongues). Just as praying in the Spirit gets us on Holy Ghost frequency so we can more easily hear from Him, it also gets us to the place where we can more easily sense Father's heart.

> *"Likewise the Spirit also helps in our weaknesses. For we do not know what we should pray for as we ought, but the Spirit*

> *Himself makes intercession for us with groanings which cannot be uttered. Now He who searches the hearts knows what the mind of the Spirit is, because He makes intercession for the saints according to the will of God."* **Romans 8:26 & 27**

As we yield to the help of the Helper, the Holy Spirit, He will pray through us, according to the will of the Father. What occurs in the Spirit when we do this can then be transitioned into English.

> *Therefore let him who speaks in a tongue pray that he may interpret. For if I pray in a tongue, my spirit prays, but my understanding is unfruitful. What is the conclusion then? I will pray with the spirit, and I will also pray with the understanding. I will sing with the spirit, and I will also sing with the understanding."* **1Corinthians 14:13-15 NKJV**

Many times in the flow of Prophetic Prayer we will just go from Tongues right into English because illumination or revelation comes, and we know what God's heart is and we know what to pray in English because it was released in Tongues.

PROPHETIC SONG / PROPHETIC WORSHIP – SOME MAY also refer to Prophetic Song as the SONG OF THE LORD or SINGING IN THE SPIRIT. Here are texts of scripture we can use to lay a doctrinal foundation.

> *"Let the word of Christ richly dwell within you, with all wisdom teaching and admonishing one another with **psalms** and **hymns** and **spiritual songs**, **singing** with thankfulness in your hearts to God."* **Colossians 3:16 NASB** (Emphasis Mine)

> *"Speaking to one another in **psalms** and **hymns** and **spiritual songs**, **singing** and making melody with your heart to the Lord."* **Ephesians 5:19 NASB** (Emphasis Mine)

> *"What is the outcome then? I shall pray with the spirit, and I shall pray with the mind also; I shall **sing** with the **spirit**, and I shall **sing** with the mind also."* **1Corinthians 14:15 NASB** (Emphasis Mine)

> *"What is the outcome then brethren? When you assemble, each one has a **psalm**, has a teaching, has a revelation, has a tongue, has an interpretation. Let all things be done for edification."* **1Corinthians 14:26 NASB** (Emphasis Mine)

It could rightly be stated that PROPHETIC SONG would be the SPIRIT OF PROPHECY expressing the thoughts and desires of Christ in song. It is important to remember when considering this point that just as Prophecy can be spoken, it can also be sung. I personally like this definition, that it is a spontaneous, unrehearsed song given by the inspiration of the Holy Spirit to either praise the Lord in worship, or to edify His Body.

SPECIAL AREAS OF THE PROPHETIC 105

Any believer may participate in PROPHETIC SONG. Of course it is more pleasing to the human ear if the one singing it actually has musical ability and can sing, therefore it is better for those with musical ability to operate this way. In addition, there will be a much stronger or heavier anointing when the song comes through a prophet or someone who regularly exercises the Gift of Prophecy.

A person who gets songs of the Lord regularly and is anointed for music ministry is called a PSALMIST. Just the same as there can be a spirit of prophecy in a room from someone with a strong prophetic gifting, enabling others to prophesy with ease; so there can be a strong anointing for the prophetic song from someone with a strong psalmist gifting, enabling others to sing the song of the Lord with ease.

RIGHT ALONG WITH PROPHETIC SONG, AND CLOSELY related to it would be PROPHETIC WORSHIP. The difference between the two would be that in PROPHETIC SONG, it would be more directed to the congregation as a message that is sung to the people from God; whereas PROPHETIC WORSHIP would be a song of worship to God that is born of the Spirit.

PROPHETIC WORSHIP can be described as: Unrehearsed, Unplanned, Spirit-led, Spontaneous, Free-flowing, Inspired, Overflowing, Progressive, and/or Building. Many times in our worship times we have to start somewhere and in the process of our worship we transition into another flow or stream. As we yield to that new flow or stream we have crossed from planned worship to PROPHETIC WORSHIP.

PROPHETIC WORSHIP is catching the wind of the Holy Spirit for a specific service and flowing with it. It could also be said that PROPHETIC WORSHIP is something that happens naturally – the Lord takes you deeper into His heart. I once described it like this when teaching along these lines: PROPHETIC WORSHIP is worship where we make room for God's voice and His manifest presence among us. Simply put, we invite God into our service for a two-way conversation.

PROPHETIC WORSHIP is where the Worship Leaders are less in tune with their guitars and more in tune with what the Holy Spirit is saying. PROPHETIC WORSHIP is where the New Songs and New Sounds from Heaven are Birthed and Released. Over and over in the Psalms we are told to sing to the Lord a New Song. *Those new songs come out in Prophetic Worship.*

THE SAME WAY THAT PEOPLE WHO DON'T NORMALLY prophesy can prophesy when the spirit of prophecy is present or being under the anointing of an extraordinarily strong prophetic gift, so you can flow in prophetic song when that strong psalmist anointing is present.

Sometimes prophetic songs are referred to as singing in the Spirit. Singing in the Spirit corporately can release a marvelous presence of God and change the spiritual atmosphere of a service as tremendous freedom comes as a result of the release of those songs of the Lord.

In the same was as with PROPHETIC PRAYER, many times the gateway into prophetic worship is singing in the Spirit (Tongues).

> *"What is the outcome then? I will pray with the spirit, and I will pray with the mind also; I will sing with the spirit, and I will sing with the mind also."* **1Corinthians 14:15 NASB**

Notice Paul said, *"I will sing with the spirit, and I will sing with the mind also."* So we need to get comfortable with both praying in tongues and singing in tongues as there are deeper moves or dimensions of the Spirit that are tied to them both. By utilizing them, we can be launched into both PROPHETIC PRAYER and PROPHETIC WORSHIP.

PROPHETIC EVANGELISM - THIS SEEMS TO BE THE NEWEST area of the Prophetic Movement that God is releasing. In essence it is taking prophetic gifting out of the church house and into the street. This scripture in 1Corinthians 14 is fairly well known for its operation in the church. PROPHETIC EVANGELISM says it can also be done not just in the church, but also out in the street.

> *"But if all **prophesy**, and an ungifted man enters, he is **convicted** by all, he is **called to account** by all; the **secrets of his heart are disclosed**; and so **he will fall on his face and worship God**, declaring that God is certainly among you."* **1Corinthians 14:24 & 25 NASB** (Emphasis Mine)

The same as we prophesy the word of the Lord to each other in church with accuracy (commonly referred to as reading people's mail), we can prophesy to people out in the street as well with accuracy (reading their mail), and they will know that God is among us, and they will worship Him.

> *"And since we have gifts that differ according to the grace given to us, let each exercise them accordingly: if prophecy, according to the proportion of his faith."* **Romans 12:6 NASB**

We know that we prophesy according to the proportion of our faith. If we can have faith for it in church, why can't we have faith for it out of the church? Let us develop our faith in this area, as it will be a great tool of evangelism for us.

Unrealistic Expectations Of The Prophetic

In the day in which we live Prophetic Ministry has gained much wider acceptance. However, I believe that many have unrealistic expectations of Prophets and Prophetic Gifting. They suppose that Prophets will always have a 'WORD' for them, and that they will always have full understanding of everything that they prophesy. I most assuredly can say that nothing could be further from the truth. Can we please examine the scriptures to see if they bear these modern thoughts out?

> *"The **prophets who prophesied** of the grace [divine blessing] which was intended for you, **searched, and inquired earnestly about this salvation**. They sought [to find out] to whom or when this was to come which the **Spirit of Christ working within them indicated** when **He predicted** the sufferings of Christ and the glories that should follow [them]. **It was then***

> ***disclosed to them** that **the services they were rendering were not meant for themselves and their period of time, but for you**. [It is these very] things which have now already been made known plainly to you by those who preached the good news (the Gospel) to you **by the [same] Holy Spirit sent from heaven**. Into these things [the very] angels long to look!"* **1Peter 1:10-12 AMPC** (Emphasis Mine)

In these three verses of scripture, three things stand out to me about Prophetic Ministry: First, it is **Spirit Inspired**, Second, it is **Supernaturally Revealed**, Third, it is **Surprisingly Limited**. I would like for us to consider each one of these three points in relation to common thoughts of today about the prophetic. As opposed to having Unrealistic Expectations, I would much rather that we have Realistic Expectations of the prophetic.

One of the most basic rules of correct Bible interpretation is to determine who was speaking as well as who they were speaking about. In this case Peter, one of the Apostles of the Lamb is speaking, and he is talking about all of the Old Covenant Prophets. So we must look at this text as if we are trying to learn something about prophetic ministry by looking at the Old Covenant Prophets.

Our first point is that prophetic ministry must be Spirit inspired. Please allow me to direct your attention to some select sections of the text which we are using from the Amplified Classic Bible.

> In verse 11 of the text it states: "...***the Spirit of Christ working within them indicated*** *when* ***He predicted*** *the sufferings of Christ and the glories that should follow...*"

> In verse 12 of the text it states: "*[It is these very] things which have now already been made known plainly to you by those who preached the good news (the Gospel) to you* ***by the [same] Holy Spirit sent from heaven...***"

We must remember that if the Spirit is not inspiring, there can be no "REAL" Prophetic Word. Just as The Spirit of God is a Prophetic Spirit, so all the Prophetic Gifts: Prophecy, Tongues, the Interpretation of Tongues, the Word of Knowledge, and the Word of Wisdom operate as the Spirit of God wills (see 1Corinthians 12:11). So none of these manifestations of the Spirit can operate apart from His inspiration.

Our second point is that prophetic ministry must be Supernaturally Revealed! Again, allow me to direct your attention to sections of the text we are using.

> In verse 11 of the text it states: "... ***the Spirit of Christ working within them indicated*** *when* ***He predicted*** *the sufferings of Christ and the glories...*"

In verse 12 of the text it states: "...*It was then* ***disclosed to them... by the [same] Holy Spirit...***"

Prophecy is always supernatural revelation; it is never things known in the natural. Did you notice that the Spirit of Christ was working in them? It was the Spirit that indicated. It was the Spirit that predicted. Yes, the prophets were the ones prophesying, **but it was the Spirit** that was giving them the revelation. Did you notice that it was disclosed (revealed) to them by the same Spirit?

It might serve us in understanding that ***it was God through the Prophet*** Amos that this declaration was made:

> *"Surely the Lord God will do nothing, but He revealeth His secret unto His servants the prophets."* **Amos 3:7 KJV**

As Holy Spirit is a Supernatural Spirit, the only way we can have True Revelation of the Spirit is that it be revealed Supernaturally!

Our third point is that prophetic ministry is SURPRISINGLY LIMITED. Again much of the thinking of today regarding the prophetic believe that just because a Prophet prophesied it, they know all the details and the timing of when these things will be. Is that accurate? Again, allow me to direct your attention to sections of the text we are using.

In verse 10 of the text it states: *"... **searched and inquired earnestly** about this salvation."*

In Verse 11 of the text it states: *"...**They sought [to find out] to whom or when this was to come**..."*

Just because someone prophesies, does not mean they fully understand all they are prophesying. Did you notice that the Prophets searched and inquired earnestly? Did you notice that they sought to find out to whom or when this was to come? It doesn't sound to me like they knew the details of what they were prophesying!

These are Prophets that wrote scripture, and they did not understand what they prophesied meant. It sounds to me like it was indeed Surprisingly Limited! We might do well to remember, especially with Prophets, that many times they speak both by Inspiration and by Revelation.

This means that often the Word of Knowledge and/or the Word of Wisdom, or both are released through the vehicle of Prophecy. The reason the Gift of the Word of Knowledge and the Gift of the Word of Wisdom are called "WORD" is because they are just that. A word. Not all of God's knowledge or wisdom…just a word of it. Again, Surprisingly Limited.

Many times what we do when we receive a Prophetic Word is go to the Prophet that gave it and demand that they tell us more, and explain the word to us fully. We cannot go to the vessel and expect more than what they revealed because either they don't know, or they are not released to say. This is referred to as PROPHETIC DISCRETION. If one does want to know more than what was revealed they should do as the old hymn says: "Take It To The Lord In Prayer."

We need to have a balanced approach to Prophetic Ministry and Prophetic Gifting. We should always desire it and not disallow it as we discussed earlier. However, we should never expect more from it than God is willing to reveal at the time it is given. Trying to go beyond God's revelation has led many into speculation, familiar spirits, and error. We certainly don't want to do that!

Sonship: A Missing Element In The Prophetic

I believe that a major missing element in the modern prophetic movement is Sonship! Many in the prophetic have not been fathered nor raised up by a seasoned Prophetic Elder. It seems we have forgotten the law of Genesis, which states that everything produces after its kind. If I plant apple seeds, I will not grow an orange tree, I will grow an apple tree, because that is the kind of seed I planted.

I am amazed at so many that want to develop in the prophetic and serve in a local church where the Pastor doesn't operate in the prophetic, nor do they allow it to operate in their services. Dear one, can I just tell you that you will not develop in your prophetic gifting in that kind of environment? To really develop in the prophetic, it is much easier if one is under a strong, mature, seasoned prophetic mantle. It really does make one's development so much easier, as well as accelerating it.

We really do need more mature prophetic mothers and fathers to arise and pour into up-and-coming prophetic voices and those with blossoming prophetic gifts. We would see a great deal less of what I call 'Granola Christianity' (things that are fruity, flakey, and nutty) in our prophetic streams if we had mature, seasoned mothers and fathers pouring into sons and daughters. Many today consider fathering an apostolic function, but I wish to remind you, Dear Reader, that apostles along with prophets together make up the foundation that the Church is built upon.

I WANT TO TALK TO BOTH FROM SOME OF MY EXPERIENCE and from some Biblical perspective regarding sonship, showing that it is also part of the prophetic, not just the apostolic. In fact, Sonship was God's idea from the beginning. It was His original intent, and is so much bigger than either the apostolic or prophetic. I am going into some of my notes and teachings from years ago when I was really beginning to embrace sonship while functioning as a prophet. I want to talk to you about **SONSHIP FROM A PROPHETIC PERSPECTIVE.**

Can we start by laying this as a foundation? The Office one stands in dictates how they view things. Apostles look at things apostolically. Prophets look at things prophetically, etcetera. As one that functioned for sixteen years as a Prophet, and still having very strong prophetic tendencies as the prophetic grace and gift is still very much a part of my life, I've just had an apostolic grace and gift added to it. But, I still tend to look at things from a Prophetic perspective. If you will, it is the colored lens of the sunglasses I look through.

If I am wearing sunglasses with red lenses, everything I look at looks red. If I am wearing sunglasses with blue lenses, everything I look at looks blue. So the color of the lenses determine how we see what we see. In the same way, the office or function we stand in colors or determines how we see what we see. So when I look at Sonship…many times I still to this day look at it from a prophetic perspective.

As I grew up, I was raised in Sonship before I knew what it was, never mind understood it. I was raised in the home of two Apostles. *(even though Mom and Dad were not functioning as apostles when I grew up, they still had apostolic tendencies long before any of us knew what apostles were, or that they still existed today.)* If you will, we are going to take *A PROPHET'S VIEW OF AN APOSTOLIC FUNCTION.*

LET'S LOOK AT SEVERAL WELL-KNOWN PASSAGES OF scripture from one of my favorite stories and encounters in the Bible. They beautifully show and demonstrate both sonship and prophets, I am talking about Elijah and Elisha.

> "The Lord said to him, 'Go, return on your way to the wilderness of Damascus, and when you have arrived, you shall anoint Hazael king over Aram; and Jehu the son of Nimshi you shall anoint king over Israel; and **Elisha the son of Shaphat of Abel-meholah you shall anoint as prophet in your place.**'" **1 Kings 19: 15 & 16 NASB** (Emphasis Mine)

> "Elijah left there and found Elisha son of Shaphat as he was plowing. Twelve teams of oxen were in front of him, and he was with the twelfth team. Elijah walked by him and threw his mantle over him. Elisha left the oxen, ran to follow Elijah, and said, 'Please let me kiss my father and mother, and then I will follow you.' 'Go on back,' he replied, 'for what have I done to you?' So he turned back from following him, took the team of oxen, and slaughtered them. With the oxen's wooden yoke and plow, he cooked the meat and gave it to the people, and they ate. **Then he left, followed Elijah, and served him.**" **1 Kings 19: 19-21 HCSB** (Emphasis Mine)

> "As they were going along and talking, behold, there appeared a chariot of fire and horses of fire which separated the two of them. And Elijah went up by a whirlwind to heaven. Elisha saw it and cried out, '**My father, my father**, the chariots of Israel and its horsemen!' And he saw Elijah no more. Then he took hold of his own clothes and tore them in two pieces." **2 Kings 2:11-13 NASB** (Emphasis Mine)

When we first encounter these two men it is in 1 Kings 19. God tells Elijah to go anoint Elisha as Prophet in his place *(or in your room other translations say)*. We must remember that during Elijah's day they already had the Sons of the Prophets and the schools of the prophets. There were those who were being trained and developed to be prophets. However, Elijah was not involved in raising the next generation. As the major Prophet at that time he was not raising a successor. So God had to give Elijah a course correction to get him on God's program to raise up a Son, someone to carry his mantle and call.

One of the greatest travesties in the Church today is ministry sons not being raised up by ministry leaders/father. The leader dies and goes on to their eternal reward, and the work/ministry dies with them because they did not have a son that they raised up that knew what they knew, and could do what they did. Someone once said that any success without a successor is a failure. Someone else said that every number one must have a number two.

Even though Elijah was a Prophet, God wanted him to have a Son...a Successor...one that could carry on his ministry. So, Elijah comes to Elisha and throws his mantle (signifying his office, call and anointing as Prophet) over the shoulders of Elisha. Elisha knew what this meant and what it signified, so he asked if he could say goodbye to his Mom and Dad properly. He knew he had to follow the man of God.

I am always amused at how Elijah acted so nonchalantly as he kept walking saying: *"What did I do?"* Then the most interesting thing...Elisha gets him to stay. Then Elisha slaughtered 12 yoke of oxen (his inheritance). Now there was nothing to go back to, there was no Plan B, and cooked the meat by throwing a feast. Finally, Elisha follows Elijah and serves him (HCSB—some translations say *ministered to him*). (The original Hebrew means *became a servant*).

By the time we get from 1Kings 19 to 2Kings 2 when Elijah will eventually be taken from him, much has changed. I have read and heard different Bible scholars say that the time period between when Elisha first followed Elijah and served him to the time that Elijah was taken up from him was anywhere from seven or eight years to 12 or 13 years. In either case, that is quite a length of time that Elisha was walking with Elijah,

It is interesting as Elijah and Elisha approach each of the locations that they come to enroute to the place where they will finally be separated, the Sons of the Prophets in each location say the same thing: *"Don't you know the Lord will take your master from you today?"* Elisha responded at each location exactly the same as he is questioned by the sons of the prophets. *"Yes I know it. Be quiet!"* (Mike Translation, *Yeah I know…SHUT UP!)*

So the Sons of the Prophets were operating by revelation as was Elisha. They knew that Elijah was going to be taken from him, but so did Elisha. Elisha during his time of serving has grown from the man with the mantle thrown over him to a man that was now operating by revelation.

It is at this point that Elijah asks Elisha: *"What do you want me to do for you?"* Now here is where the story gets interesting. Elisha responds that he wants a double portion of Elijah's spirit. *(Now I have been hearing for many years that this is why Elisha did twice as many miracles as Elijah did, and it is true that he did, I do not believe that was his motivation for this request.)* Elijah responds that he has asked a hard thing but if you see me when I am taken from you it shall be granted.

I have heard some expound from the Hebrew that what Elijah responds to Elisha here means more than just seeing him when he is taken, but actually infers if we are seeing eye to eye, or that you are seeing like I see, it will be done for you. This would certainly carry a much deeper meaning than just seeing him as he is taken.

Now comes the separation where Elijah is taken from Elisha. As the chariot comes in the whirlwind to take Elijah, Elisha sees it and cries out: *"My Father, my Father, the chariot of Israel and the horsemen."* Did you notice that Elisha did not say – My Mentor, My Mentor. He did not say – My Teacher, My Teacher. He did not say My Prophet, My Prophet *(even though he was all of those things).* He said – My Father. My Father! Yes, even Prophets Need Fathers!

Somewhere in the process of Elisha walking with Elijah, that was either seven or eight years to possibly 12 or 13 years, Elisha went from Servant to Son! Back to the importance of the double portion request. Why did Elisha ask for a double portion of Elijah's spirit? It was sonship talk! Say What?! What do you mean by SONSHIP TALK?

WE MUST REMEMBER THE CUSTOM OF THE DAY WHEN Elijah and Elisha lived in Israel's history. If a man had four sons and died, his inheritance was not divided equally among his four sons, where each got 25% of their father's inheritance. Rather it would be divided where the first-born son would get 40%, and then the other three sons would each get 20%. Why is that? Because the first-born son got a double portion. Then the rest would be divided evenly. When Elisha asked for the double portion, he was asking for the first-born son's portion! Hence he asked for a double portion.

You know how the story goes, it is at this point that Elijah's mantle falls and Elisha picks it up. Okay…wait a minute. I thought when Elijah called Elisha he threw his mantle over Elisha's shoulders?! Well, he did. So then, if it was thrown over his shoulders back at their first encounter, why was he not carrying it? Why did it need to fall in order for him to pick it up?

It is obvious that Elijah threw [the mantle] signifying the Call of God to stand in the office of Prophet as his successor. But when it fell, and Elisha now picked it up, it signified the Commission of Elisha that he was ready to carry the weight of the office of Prophet that Elijah walked in.

We must learn that there is a huge difference between the Call of God and the Commission of God! I hear over and over again these days that I am Called, or that I have the Call of God on my life. My normal reply is: *"Congratulations, the process is about to begin!"*

The Bible says that many are called but few are chosen (see Matthew 22:14). The time between the Call of God and the Commission of God is called the Process. *(Some folks think process is a Christian cuss word because we hate process.)* But there is no way to get from the Call to the Commission without it.

So now Elisha picks up the mantle and asks: *"Where is the Lord God of Elijah?"* as he approaches the same Jordan River that he had just crossed with his Father and strikes the water and again it separates just as it had done when he and Elijah crossed it just a bit ago. It is at this point that the sons of the Prophets that are watching declare: *"The spirit of Elijah rests on Elisha!"* He didn't just get his physical mantle. He got what it represented, the spiritual mantle of his father Elijah.

I WISH AT THIS POINT TO LOOK AT ANOTHER FAMILIAR portion of scripture from the Prophet Malachi.

> *"Behold, I am going to send you* **Elijah the prophet** *before the coming of the great and terrible day of the Lord.* **He will restore the hearts of the fathers to their children and the hearts of the children to their**

> ***fathers***, *so that I will not come and smite the land with a curse."* **Malachi 4: 5 & 6 NASB** (Emphasis Mine)

Notice in this text the Prophet Malachi prophesies about the coming of Elijah the Prophet. After he speaks of the coming of the Prophet Elijah, he speaks about the hearts of fathers turned to sons, and then sons to fathers. This is speaking of a restoration to take place of those that would operate prophetically in the spirit of Elijah, which in turn would release the fathering anointing of hearts of Fathers turned to children…and children to fathers.

I fully believe that when Malachi was prophesying about the coming of Elijah, he of course was not talking about reincarnation, but rather one that would come in the spirit and power of Elijah. I believe that this prophetic word had a first fulfillment as scripture clearly indicates in the Gospel narrative in the Life of Jesus speaking about John The Baptist (see Luke 1:17).

I believe there is also a second fulfillment of Malachi's prophecy referring to the current Prophetic and Apostolic Restoration moves of God in the earth. If you have studied these moves of restoration you will know that we have been in a season that has been a fulfillment of Peter's message in Acts, Chapter 3.

> *"Therefore repent and return, so that your sins may be wiped away, in order that times of refreshing may come from the presence of the Lord; and that He may send Jesus, the Christ appointed for you,* ***whom heaven must receive until the period of restoration of all things about which***

***God spoke by the mouth of His holy prophets** from ancient time."* **Acts 3: 19-21 NASB** (Emphasis Mine)

Here Peter preaching, speaks about a time period called the restoration of all things spoken by the mouth of His holy Prophets. Everything must be restored that the Prophets had declared. Everything that once was or existed in the church needed to be restored. In the early church (Ephesians, chapter 4), there were five ministry offices in the Church. Apostle, Prophet, Evangelist, Pastor, and Teacher. About 100 years or so ago, there was one. The Pastor only.

Since the late 1940s, the church has been experiencing several works of restoration of the other four Ascension Gifts that were lost to the church through the passage of time.

From the late 40s – the mid 50s God restored the office of Evangelist with the Voice of Healing Revival. We saw people like AA Allen, Oral Roberts, William Branham, Jack Coe, etcetera rise and come on the scene.

In the 1970s God restored the office of the Teacher with the Word of Faith movement. We saw people like Kenneth E. Hagin, Kenneth Copeland, Charles Capps, Fred Price, Marilyn Hickey, etcetera rise and come on the scene.

In the Late 80s – mid 90s God restored the office of the Prophet with what has been called the Prophetic Movement. We saw people like Bill Hamon, Chuck

Pierce, James Goll, Cindy Jacobs, etcetera rise and come on the scene.

In the mid 90s – the 2000's God restored the office of the Apostle with what has been called the Apostolic Movement. We saw people like C. Peter Wagner, Che Ahn, John Kelly, Jonas Clark, etcetera rise and come on the scene.

These restoration works that the Church has lived through over these years have set the stage, as we are currently living in what Peter termed 'the restoration of all things.' We are now ready for what Malachi prophesied, that the hearts of the fathers would be turned to the sons, and the sons to the fathers.

Prophet Malachi prophesied it, and we are watching it. The Apostolic and Prophetic Movements have restored it. Yes, John the Baptist was the first fulfillment, but now we are living in the second. We are witnessing Fathers turning their hearts toward Sons. Notice, Sons don't turn their hearts towards Fathers until Fathers first turn their hearts toward the Sons.

We see this in our day. I am living proof! As I wrote in my book, *From Father To Son: An Example Of Multigenerational Sonship* (released in 2022), I was fathered by my earthly father, and now I am pouring into others even as he poured into me. Malachi prophesied that this would come, and it has!

I wrote a statement at the beginning of this chapter:

"I believe that a major missing element in the modern prophetic movement is sonship!"

This should no longer be! If Elijah could Father and raise up his replacement in Elisha…If we are in the days of the restoration of all things…If the hearts of the fathers are being turned to the sons, then there is no reason that we should have this missing element! We just need the Fathers and the Sons to rise up into their place, recognizing and fulfilling their respective roles.

The Synergistic Working Of Apostles & Prophets

Let us begin this last chapter of the book by restating three foundational scriptures that we have already looked at in this manuscript multiple times.

*"And He gave some as **apostles**, and some as **prophets**, and some as **evangelists**, and some as **pastors** and **teachers**."* **Ephesians 4:11 NASB** (Emphasis Mine)

*"And God has appointed in the church, **first apostles**, **second prophets**, third teachers, then miracles, then gifts of healings, helps, administrations, various kinds of tongues."* **1 Corinthians 12:28 NASB** (Emphasis Mine)

*"Having been built on the **foundation of the apostles and prophets**, Christ Jesus Himself being the corner stone."* **Ephesians 2:20 NASB** (Emphasis Mine)

In all three of the texts listed above we see that these two offices are linked together. It seems like through much of the New Testament we see a linking of Apostles and Prophets together. The gift of Apostle along with the gift of the Prophet together makes up the foundation that the church is built upon (See Ephesians 2:20 above).

God's true Apostles and Prophets are not in competition with each other. They were designed by Christ to complement each other. They are the only two of the five Ascension Gifts (or five-fold ministry) that are paired together in ministry by name in this way.

> *"As I briefly wrote earlier, God himself revealed his mysterious plan to me. As you read what I have written, you will understand my insight into this plan regarding Christ. God did not reveal it to previous generations,* **but now by his Spirit he has revealed it to his holy apostles and prophets.***"*
> **Ephesians 3:3-5 NLT** (Emphasis Mine)

It is God's pre-ordained will for Apostles and Prophets to work together. These two gifts (Apostles and Prophets) are like a team of two horses harnessed together and pulling one wagonload of anointed ministry. Dr C. Peter Wagner in his writings would declare that he loved the analogy of Apostles being **hitched** to Prophets…he would explain that Apostles could do certain good things on their own, and that Prophets could do certain good things on their own, but hitched together they could change the world!

In looking at the New Testament it seems that there are two types of Apostle-Prophet relationships. First, there would seem to be a CASUAL RELATIONSHIP – much like that of Apostle Paul and Prophet Agabus, they were acquainted with each other, their paths did cross, but they did not travel together. We could say that they were 'tied-together', but did not work closely together.

The second type of relationship would seem to be a STRUCTURED RELATIONSHIP—much like that of Apostle Paul and Prophet Silas. They obviously had a much closer relationship [than Paul and Agabus had] as Silas was Paul's traveling partner and ministry companion. They are a great example of the biblical linking of Apostles and Prophets that we would consider as being **harnessed together.**

It is clear from examining these two types of relationships that both of them involved an Apostle and a Prophet, but clearly the dynamics of both relationships were vastly different. I really like thinking of it as a CASUAL RELATIONSHIP where they were **tied-together,** versus a STRUCTURED RELATIONSHIP where they were **harnessed together**.

Another New Testament example of an Apostle and a Prophet being linked together, although not too commonly thought of, would be Jesus and John the Baptist. Yes, Jesus certainly was a Prophet as well as all of the other ministry gifts. He was definitely an Apostle too.

The Synergistic Working Of Apostles & Prophets

> *"Therefore, holy brethren, partakers of the heavenly calling, consider the **Apostle** and High Priest of our confession, Christ Jesus."* **Hebrews 3:1** (Emphasis Mine)

And I believe it would certainly go without a doubt that John the Baptist was a Prophet.

> *"For I say to you, among those born of women **there is not a greater prophet than John the Baptist**; but he who is least in the kingdom of God is greater than he."* **Luke 7:28** (Emphasis Mine)

THE OFFICES OF APOSTLE AND PROPHET HAVE BEEN joined together by Almighty God, and what God has joined together, let no man put asunder *(separate or divide)*. Of course I am stealing the verbiage that a minister would normally recite at a wedding of a man and woman. The minister will very often say after the exchange of the marriage vows: *"What God has joined together let not man put asunder."* Even as God has joined the man and woman together in holy matrimony, He has joined the Apostle and Prophet together in ministry.

In order for both the Apostle and Prophet to have maximum impact and effectiveness, they must **synergistically** work together. It would really help if we dove into this word 'synergistically' to get the full import of this statement.

This word comes from the root word synergism - *interaction of discrete agencies (as industrial firms), agents (as drugs), or conditions such that the total effect is greater than the sum of the individual effects.* **Webster's Dictionary.**

This word really came to popularity in the health supplement industry regarding the use of vitamins. Many were just popping handfuls of pills randomly, but after much research they discovered that it was better to have certain vitamins paired together in certain doses known as "SYNERGISTIC COMPOUNDS," which gave the user the maximum impact and benefit from the supplements they took.

So it is with the offices of Apostle and Prophet. When they are synergistically linked, there is maximum impact from their combined or joined ministry together that is not felt or recognized when they minister alone! The mutual ministries of Apostles and Prophets is unique because they have so many things in common in their abilities and function, yet they are interdependent on each other rather than independent of each other. There is no competition between them, but ration a completion between them. Their callings, ministries, and destinies are linked together. Each gives the other respect and honor so that both have acceptance and appreciation for and from the other.

IN THE LINKING OF APOSTLES AND PROPHETS, SOMETIMES my mind goes back to some Saturday morning cartoons from my childhood, and I think of the "Wonder-Twins" or "Power-Twins." It is a paradox that they are unique, the same, and different at the same time, yet when working together they both fulfill their goals and ministries, even if operating slightly differently.

Back in the 90's when both the Apostolic and Prophetic Restorations where in full swing, God used two of His men as pioneers to be a living picture for the church of a Paul/Silas type of relationship where an Apostle and Prophet were synergistically linked. That pairing was the partnership of Apostle C. Peter Wagner and Prophet Chuck Pierce. It was a great picture of a structured type of relationship.

At this point in our discussion it would serve us well to define the principles of the Apostle/Prophet relationship. First of all, when the prophetic revelation of a Prophet is combined with the wisdom of an Apostle, there is a whole new level of strategic application. The insights Prophets receive into God's strategy and timing for nations, cities, and people are an incredible help to an Apostolic Church. The combination of prophetic anointing and the signs and wonders that accompany apostolic ministry creates an incredible atmosphere for Kingdom advancement.

Even in a Paul/Agabus type relationship it is critical that Apostles be open to receiving prophetic ministry from proven Prophets with whom they are NOT in a team relationship. *In fact many times a Prophet who is not intimately acquainted with a person's life can speak more accurately because the*

WORD *is not affected by their natural knowledge.* Through the prophetic gift(s) they operate by, Prophets can bring to Apostles revelation that is vital to their ministry; whether it is a warning, encouragement or comfort. This aspect of the Prophet's ministry cannot be minimized.

One of the hardest of all relationships to successfully navigate is the relationship between peers. Even though God has set Apostles in the church first, Prophets many times will also be peers and even intimate friends. In my case it was family members. For 16 years of my ministry I functioned as a Prophet while my parents were functioning as Apostles. When this is the case mutual respect, humility, and submission to one another are even more critical. **The fruitfulness of Apostles and Prophets can increase exponentially when they are willing to work as a team.** Whether it is the revelation provided by the Prophet, or the wisdom and governmental grace of the Apostle, these ministries have an ability to complement one another that is unique in the Kingdom of God.

C. PETER WAGNER IN HIS WRITINGS SPEAKING ALONG this line said: *"If Apostles are properly hitched to Prophets, if they have established a covenant relationship and if they have agreed to pull together in ministry, a repeatable pattern emerges."*[1]

This would be the proposed pattern or cycle of the Apostle/Prophet relationship. First the Prophet would submit to the Apostle recognizing that New Testament Government indicates that the Apostle was set first, while the Prophet is the 'other of two', like unto the first. *This is not like what the shepherding movement did, and we are also not talking about big-headed folks on a power trip, but rather Biblical submission that understands Biblical order.*

Second would be that God would speak to the Prophet, usually in line with the way He normally speaks to them, whether that be Nabi or Seer. [This is not to say that God cannot speak to an Apostle. He does, but the Prophet has been delegated primarily to hear from God and be His mouthpiece. The Prophet must also make sure they are getting the accurate message of God for the moment and not mix it with self.]

Next, the Prophet would speak to the Apostle regarding the revelation that they have received. It is the Prophet's responsibility to convey to the Apostle what they have received. It is at this point that they must exercise PROPHETIC DISCRETION, knowing what to tell *and* what not to tell. Many times the Prophet will know more than they are released to say. Not everything they know is to be communicated. Only what they are released to say.

Now, it is up to the Apostle to judge and evaluate what they have received from the Prophet so they can strategize and execute it. Once the prophetic word has been given to the Apostle, the burden for serious discernment switches from the Prophet to the Apostle. It is up to the Apostle now to pray over this revelation to see how and when God wants it implemented.

(Remember every revelation has a timing, it is not always immediate).

Once the Apostle has the action plan and implements the revelation, the cycle is complete, and starts all over again, where the Prophet submits to the Apostle, getting the next instruction from God.

---

1. C. Peter Wagner, *Apostles and Prophets: The Foundation of the Church* (Ventura, CA: Gospel Light Publications, 2000), p. 88. (Kindle edition).

Final Thoughts

There is no way that one book can cover everything that there is about any given subject. But this writing is the most in-depth and exhaustive manuscript I have released to date. I have incorporated all of the areas of the Prophetic that I have expertise and experience in, having written several syllabi and been teaching for over 20 years.

I think that there might be a comparison to the summation written at the end of John's Gospel to what is found in these pages.

> *"And truly Jesus did many other signs in the presence of His disciples, which are not written in this book;* **but these are written that you may believe** *that Jesus is the Christ, the Son of God, and that believing you may have life in His name."* **John 20: 30-31 NKJV** (Emphasis Mine)

There was no way that John could have included everything that Jesus said or did. But he included what he did so people might believe. Similarly, there was no way I could include everything about the Prophetic in one book, but these things were included so that you might believe; that Prophets, Prophecy, and Prophetic Gifting are still for the New Testament Church today!

It is also my hope and intention in writing this book that maybe some correction will come to the Body of Christ. And that maybe we will get some things back in order resembling the pattern of the writings in the Epistles of how these things should look, function, and operate in Ekklesia *(that is decently and in order)*.

About the Author

At this writing Michael Fram is a second-generation Teacher & Preacher concluding his 44th year and approaching his 45th year of active ministry. Through the years he has functioned as:

- An Evangelist
- A Bible School Teacher
- A Shot-term Missionary
- A Revivalist
- A Seminar Speaker
- A Prophet
- An Overseer of a Local Fellowship
- A Blogger & Writer
- An Apostle
- A Mentor, Big Brother, & Spiritual Father

Michael carries three Ministry Mandates or Apostolic Assignments:

- Promote & Support Women in Ministry
- Pour into the Next Generation of up & coming Leaders *(do for others what his father did for him)*

- Regional Alignment – Gather Leaders together in Regions crossing:
- Generational Lines
- Denominational Lines
- Ethic Lines
- Gender Lines

For more information, please contact:

Rev. Michael Fram
Prophetic Destiny Ministries International
www.propheticdestyministriesintl.org

Find Rev. Fram on FACEBOOK:

https://www.facebook.com/PropheticDestinyMinistries

Also by Rev. Michael Fram

Kingdom Transformation - Through Ascension Gifts Working Together

What The Devil Saw On The Day Of Pentecost

From Father To Son – An Example Of Multigenerational Sonship

Available on Amazon

www.ingramcontent.com/pod-product-compliance
Lightning Source LLC
Chambersburg PA
CBHW070804100426
42742CB00012B/2247